Love

101

Love

101

by
Robert Strand

New Leaf Press

Library of Congress Catalog Number: 93-84143
ISBN: 0-89221-237-3

All Scripture quotations are from the NIV unless noted.

Contents

Dedication

To my wife Donna, and my mother, Ruth, who have already written the book on love.

Also — to Cliff Dudley, deceased, through whose interest and encouragement this book was birthed.

Introduction

It happened in a typical small-town church. It was Sunday morning service and the four-year-old class was up front to sing for the congregation as part of the worship. When they had finished, the young choir marched past the pastor, who was standing resplendent in his clerical robe. As each tiny worshiper came past, the pastor made a comment or patted him on the head. For just a moment in time, each child was the center of attention with the pastor. Somehow, though, one little boy was inadvertently missed; the pastor, for some reason, overlooked him. When the oversight had been realized by the little one, he ran crying to his mother, sobbing, "God didn't look at me . . . God didn't look at me!"

You need love. I need love. The baby boomer you see on the street needs love. Each forgotten elderly person in a nursing home needs love. The boss at your business needs love. The entertainer on TV needs love. The self-assured millionaire in your town needs love. The single parent struggling with life needs love. Everybody needs love.

If there's a dearth of any commodity in today's

high-tech world, it's love. Our society is moving rapidly toward isolation. "Cocooning" is the 90s buzzword for withdrawing into one's home. Home entertainment centers, home workout stations, personal computers and fax machines for those who work in their homes are among the top-selling appliances today. Home delivery of complete meals is on the increase. Soon, "pay-per-view" TV will make it unnecessary to go to a video rental store — you'll be able to watch a movie from a vast library just by entering a code number into your remote control.

While these innovations will make our lives more convenient, they will also further remove us from direct contact with other human beings. But is this good for us?

John Naisbitt, author of *Megatrends*, makes this observation: "Today, more than ever, there is an increased need to be in touch with people. We must learn to balance the material wonders of technology with the spiritual demands of our human nature."[1] We have entered a new and different era in human history. It's a high-tech world which will in turn demand a high-touch response. We are moving into a time of depersonalization; this in turn highlights the basic human need of being in touch with other human beings.

The need to be near others is just one aspect of a greater and deeper need in us all: the need for love. Love is basic to our very survival! There is no human being who can survive life on his or her own. We need each other, we need the love of another person, and we need to love other people.

In *Forecast 2000*, George Gallup, Jr., president of the Gallup Poll and internationally recognized expert on trends, writes this in his conclusion: "We now face serious dangers that threaten our future and perhaps our very existence as a nation. They strike at the heart of our social and political system, and if they aren't corrected soon, we'll be in for a time of devastating troubles.

"Obviously, many of these threats — nuclear disaster, environmental hazards, economic ills, family crises, and crime — aren't new. We hear about them almost every week on radio and television newscasts, and we read about them regularly in our daily newspapers. What is new is the intensity with which they demand our attention."[2]

One of the ways in which disaster in human relationships can be averted is by a return to love that is translated into action. An action-oriented love that makes a difference. That's what this book is all about.

Love is the factor that makes a home operate smoothly. Love is the oil in human relationships. Love is water, fertilizer, and sunshine for a growing church. Love is the key to making this world a pleasant place in which to live. Love is life's shock absorber. What is love? How do we love? That is the theme of this book.

The ultimate statement about love is found in God's Word from the writings of the apostle Paul in 1 Corinthians 13. We'll be basing our working definition of love on the characteristics as outlined in verses 4 through 7: "Love is patient, love is kind. It does not envy, it does not boast, it is not proud. It is not rude, it is not self-seeking, it is not easily angered, it keeps no record of wrongs. Love does not delight in evil but rejoices with the truth. It always protects, always trusts, always hopes, always perseveres."

Then, in verse 8, Paul gives the bottom line of love: "Love never fails." To never fail under any kind of circumstance or situation or with any kind of relationship is making an awesome claim!

We begin to understand love when we see it played out in the lives of others who struggle — as we do — and yet triumph. Such a story is taken from the time when Oliver Cromwell lived in England. A young soldier had been tried in military court for an infraction and had been sentenced to die. He was to be shot at the "ringing of the curfew bell."

His fiance climbed up into the bell tower several hours before curfew time was to be sounded and tied herself to the bell's huge clapper. At curfew time, when the bell was to be rung, only muted sounds came out of the bell tower. Cromwell demanded to know why the bell was not ringing. He sent some of his soldiers to investigate. They found the young woman cut and bleeding from being knocked back and forth against the great bell. When they brought her down, the story goes, Cromwell was so impressed with her love and willing- ness to suffer on behalf of someone she loved that he dismissed the soldier and his death sentence by saying, "Curfew shall not ring tonight!"

That's love in action.

Part One

What Love Is and Does

Definition: Love is an action directed to another person that is motivated by our relationship to Jesus Christ and is given freely without a personal reward in mind.

1

Love . . .
Is Patient

John Wesley was blessed with a very patient mother named Susanna. One time Wesley's father remarked, "I marvel at your patience! You have told that child the same thing twenty times!"

Susanna Wesley looked fondly at the child in need of love and correction and said, "Had I spoken the matter only nineteen times, I should have lost all my labor."

When it comes to this special quality of life called "patience," most of us are like the person who prayed, "Lord, I want patience and I want it now!"

So that all of us start on the same foundation of understanding, let's take another look at the meaning of the word "patience." According to the *Random House Dictionary*, patience is "the bearing of provocation, annoyance, misfortune, pain, etc., without complaint, loss of temper or irritation. An ability or willingness to suppress annoyance when confronted with delay. Quiet perseverance; even-tempered care; diligence: to work with patience." Wow!

Do we find the same kind of meaning in the original language in which the Bible was written? Yes. The Greek word is "*makrothumeo*," meaning "long-spirited, forbearing, or to have long patience, to patiently endure." Not exactly a common element in human relations today. We tend to snap, be short and uptight with each other.

A split second has been defined as the moment of time between the stop light turning green and the sounding of the person's horn from the car behind you. Impatience marks our world. We must have quick food, instant gratifications, fast diets, instant fixes, and easy answers. Yet the human puzzle doesn't respond well to the quick fix or the band-aid approach. Human relationships that are meaningful, satisfying, and lasting are not built overnight. Love is willing to invest whatever time it may take to gently deal with each other in our circle of life.

The very essence of what I'm attempting to say is captured in the following verse. It's too bad that the author is unknown; credit should be given for such thoughts:

> Let me be a little kinder.
> Let me be a little blinder
> To the faults of those about me;
> Let me praise a little more.

Let me be when I am weary
Just a little bit more cheery,
Let me serve a little better
Those that I am striving for.

Let me be a little braver
When temptation bids me waver;
Let me strive a little harder
To be all that I should be.

Let me be a little meeker
With the brother that is weaker,
Let me think more of my neighbor
And a little less of me.

Let me be a little sweeter,
Make my life a bit completer;
Keep me faithful to my duty
Every minute of the day.

Let me toil without complaining,
Not a humble task disdaining;
Let me face the summons calmly
When death beckons me away.

> . . . *Anonymous*

The Bible is not silent when it comes to patience as a part of the equipment needed by all of us if we are to make it in this life. "You need to be patient, in order to do the will of God and receive what He promises" (Heb. 10:36;TEV).

WE ALL NEED PATIENCE!

I don't think there is an argument against the need

of patience. We also agree that it's a beautiful and necessary quality we need in a generous portion from other people. We need to be shown patience . . . we need to show patience. The rub for most of us is how to develop patience and how to live it in our daily life.

We all want patience, but we do all we can to avoid the process of patience. How do we develop patience? Two specific things are mentioned in the Word as being instruments in the growth and development of this quality of life: *tribulation* and the *trying of your faith.*

The word "tribulation" is not too familiar with us in the twentieth century. But we can well understand the synonymous terms of trouble, problems, trials, and sufferings. We all can identify with such terms.

The proof text is found in Romans 5:3: ". . . but we glory in tribulations also: knowing that tribulation worketh patience" (KJV). The NIV renders it like this: ". . . but we also rejoice in our sufferings, because we know that suffering produces perseverance."

We want to have patience, but who wants to suffer? The line forms here — but it's a very short line. Few people say, "Please, Lord, let me suffer a while, because it feels so good and I like the end product of patience so much!"

Maybe it's a good thing that we seem to have no options about the trials, problems, troubles, and sufferings that come into our lives. We'd all avoid the process if we could. We want the product, but not the process. Yet in God's Word there are no short cuts to the development.

The apostle Paul, who it seems must have had a masters degree as well as two or three honorary doctorates in suffering (refer to 2 Cor. 11:23-33), wrote: "I am content with weaknesses, insults, hardships, persecutions, and difficulties for Christ's sake" (TEV). He then writes how God has worked tribulation in his life to the enhancing of his ministry. "The things that prove that I am an apostle were done with all patience among you" (2 Cor. 12:9,12;TEV). We could paraphrase Paul like this: "There is no easy road to patience."

WE LEARN BY LIVING

Life experience is how patience is developed within us. We go through a trial which, in turn, is tested by another trial which is tested by a third trial, and on and on. All this testing is to see if patience has become a way of life for us. We will continually be tested until the lesson has taken.

"How many pious, godly souls have been struck down through the centuries, even as they prayed for deliverance? Yet, despite all this ... despite the impossible questions, the drab and tawdry times, the failures ... we are still called upon to pray with, of all things, great expectations! An absurdity, a paradox. Yet the gospel truth.

"God, it seems, chooses to work in enigma and pain, with miracles as rare but as real as meteor flashes across a dark night." So wrote a weary Harold Myra.[1]

Maybe it will help you to know that this same Harold Myra became president of Christianity Today, Inc., one of the nation's largest publishers of theological materials. Myra learned the mercy and grace of God in suffering, mystery, weakness, and joy. At age seventeen, his brother murdered a neighbor lady and was sentenced to life in prison. His cousin, Lois, was killed in an auto accident just after receiving her nursing degree and about to begin a promising career. His cousin David's wife, a missionary nurse to Africa, died of leukemia in her prime, leaving young children mother-less. But through all this, Myra did not lose his faith in the faithful God.

God works in paradox, pain, trials, tribulations, and sufferings so that wd who are His servants will be able to relate to Him and to others near us with patience.

Working patience in us, along with tribulation, is the *trying of your faith*. The apostle James wastes no time in getting to the point. He begins his short book with only one verse of greeting, then plunges into the subject of patience in his next: "Dear brothers, is your life full of difficulties and temptations? Then be happy, for when the way is rough, your patience has a chance to grow. So let it grow, and don't try to squirm out of your problems. For when your patience is finally in full bloom, then you will be ready for anything" (James 1:2-4;LB).

James says that patience is developed when faith is tested. *Okay, so how long will I be in the testing time of my faith before I can be patient?* That all depends on how we respond to the test. Some of us are so busy attempting to squirm out of the testing that we never quite learn the lessons the testing is sent to bring about. So God plunges us back into the vat of testing once more. Some of us have not learned the very elementary lessons of what testing can teach us, so we have to go through the very same thing over and over again. Instead of seeing the big picture and submitting to the taskmaster of test, we gripe, grumble, question God, and remain pygmy in the perfecting of patience.

> *The outcome of a testing of faith is patience; and without patience, love will not be displayed as it should be.*

The testing and resulting patience of Adoniram Judson, the well-known missionary to Burma, is featured in a biography of this man of God by Courtney Anderson. Judson suffered numerous hardships in his ministry. He was thrown into Ava Prison in India for seventeen months where he was subjected to incredibly inhumane treatment. As a result of this stay, the scars made by the chains and iron shackles were visible for the rest of his life.

Anderson writes that upon Judson's release he asked for permission to go into another province where he could continue the preaching of the gospel. The godless ruler indignantly denied his request, saying, "My people are not fools enough to listen to anything a missionary might say, but I fear they might be impressed by your *scars* and turn to your religion."[2]

The outcome of a testing of faith is patience; and without patience, love will not be displayed as it should be. James concludes his book with this positive statement: "Be patient" (James 5:7; LB).

All of this is another way of saying the experiences of life cut away impatience; they replace annoyance and complaint with patience. Patience is learning how to suppress one's feelings when confronted with delay. It's putting up with another's slowness in turn. It's being able to place yourself in another's situation. Patience is a very active quality of love.

Richard Wurmbrand, in his book *Tortured for Christ*, deals with the communists' brutal treatment of Christians. He writes of one instance which depicts patience and heroism for Christ in a prison. On the pain of being severely beaten, preaching to the other prisoners was strictly forbidden.

Wurmbrand says,

A number of us decided to pay the price for the privilege, so we accepted their terms (a brutal beating for preaching). It was a deal; we preached and they beat us. We were happy preaching; they were happy beating us; so everyone was happy.

The following scene took place more times than I can remember. A brother was preaching to the other prisoners when the guards suddenly burst in, surprising him halfway through a phrase. They hauled him down the corridor to their "beating room." After what seemed an endless beating, they brought him back and threw him bruised and bloody on the prison floor. Slowly, he picked his battered body up, painfully straightened his clothing, and said, "Now brethren, where did I leave off when I was interrupted?" He continued his gospel message.

In the paraphrased words of James, "Let your patience be completed so that you may be perfect and complete in your actions of love!"

Love is . . . PATIENT!

2

Love . . . Is Kind

In the classic book, *Les Miserables*, Victor Hugo tells the story of Jean Valjean, whose only crime in life was stealing a single loaf of bread to feed his sister's starving children. Just one loaf. After serving nineteen years in prison, Valjean was released. He searched for work, but because of his prison record was unable to find any. Valjean finally made his way to the home of an elderly bishop where he was given supper and a bed for the night.

During supper, Valjean ate off of beautiful silver plates. He marveled at the fact that he, a recent prisoner, was eating from such elegant ware. As he lay in bed, he thought of their value. He got out of bed earlier than the rest of the household and, yielding to the temptation, stole the silver plates, slipping out of the house under cover of darkness. But he was soon caught by the police and returned to the bishop's home.

"This man stole your plates," said the policeman. The kind bishop told the officer, "Why, I gave them to him. And Jean, you forgot to take the candle sticks."

Jean Valjean was so overwhelmed at the bishop's display of kindness he became a Christian. This simple act of kindness brought about a complete change in his life. It's absolutely amazing what can happen in human relationships by an honest act of kindness!

Yet today it is so easy to confuse kindness with weakness. After all, who wants to take the time to be kind when there are goals to reach for and people to step on to reach the pinnacle of success? Kindness is in very short supply, while the demand has never been greater.

KINDNESS NOW

Kindness manifests itself in a good or benevolent nature toward other people. We speak of kindness with words such as humane, gentle, tender, compassionate, and gracious. It's having and showing a sympathetic attitude toward others.

The name Stephen Grellet is hardly a household word. He was a French-born Quaker who died in New Jersey in 1855. Grellet would be totally unknown to our world today except for a few lines which have made him immortal. He wrote, "I shall pass through this world but once. Any good that I can do, or any kindness that I can show to any human being, let me do it now and not defer it. For I shall not pass this way again."

Then there was the Yale University president who gave this advice regarding kindness to the president of

The Ohio State University: "Always be kind to your 'A' and 'B' students. Someday one of them will return to your campus as a good professor. And always be kind to your 'C' students. Someday one of them will return and build you a two-million dollar science laboratory."

By an act of kindness I am referring to that high sense of consideration for others that results in helping, even if it costs some sacrifice. Most of us can easily recall acts of kindness that have been given to

> *Kindness is in very short supply, while the demand has never been greater.*

us. Why? Because there have been so few of them along life's way.

One of the greatest indictments Jesus had against the religious experts of His day was their lack of kindness. In the Gospel of Luke, chapter 13, Jesus was teaching in the synagogue on the Sabbath day and noticed a woman who was crippled and bent over, probably with some kind of spinal disease or back injury. He laid His hands on her and said, "Woman, you are loosed from your infirmity." This act of kindness angered the priest who lashed out at Jesus for disregard for the traditions of the Sabbath. Let's read the answer Jesus gave:

"Hypocrite! Does not each one of you on the Sabbath loose his ox or donkey from the stall and lead it away to water it? So ought not this woman, being a daughter of Abraham, who Satan has bound — think of it — for eighteen years, be loosed from this bond on the Sabbath?" (Luke 13:10-17;NKJV).

Jesus is saying, "Be as kind to the needy, hurting human being as you would be in the treatment of your animals." These religionists were so busy keeping the very letter of the law they had no time for kindness! Yet, showing kindness is one of our greatest privileges.

I want to make a strong case for kindness. Let's take a closer look at this beautiful characteristic.

KINDNESS INCREASES THE KINGDOM OF GOD

As we track the movements and growth of the New Testament church we discover that their first and greatest strength was the power of the Holy Spirit, given at Pentecost. From this infilling, they went forth witnessing to the gospel of Jesus Christ.

But their second source of strength and influence was not in a creed or an organization, but in love and kindness! One major means of reaching unbelievers with the message of love is through acts of kindness. Love is manifested in acts of kindness.

These early Christians lifted a page directly from the lifestyle of their Master. They had seen Him stop a funeral procession and raise back to life a widow's son . . . they had watched as He stooped to write in the sand before the accusers of a woman caught in adultery . . . they had seen Him pick up little children to hold them in His arms . . . they had seen the look of love as He pleaded for the multitudes to come to Him . . . they were there as He invited Zacchaeus to come down from his tree and much, much more. Love was shown through kind acts.

KINDNESS KINDLES HOPE

The kind word spoken to the unruly child may do more to stop wrong behavior than any other action. The kind deed done by an employer on behalf of the slowest worker will do more to make him or her a productive asset to the company. The kindness shown to one who is away from God may do more to bring him or her to the kingdom of God than all the preaching in the world.

Tears glistened in the eyes of the Salvation Army officer, Captain Shaw, as he looked at the three men before him. Shaw was a Salvation Army medical missionary who had just arrived in India to take over a leper colony. These three men had manacles and fetters binding their hands and feet, cutting their diseased flesh. Captain Shaw turned to the guard and said, "Please unfasten the chains."

"It isn't safe," the guard replied. "These men are dangerous criminals as well as lepers!"

"I'll be responsible. They're suffering enough," Captain Shaw said, as he put out his hand and took the keys, removed the shackles, and treated their bleeding ankles and wrists.

About two weeks later Captain Shaw had his first misgivings about freeing these criminals. He had to make an overnight trip and dreaded leaving his wife and child alone. His wife insisted that she wasn't afraid — after all, God was there.

The next morning she went to the front door and was startled to see the three criminal lepers lying on her steps.

"Why are you here?" she inquired.

One of the lepers explained, "We know the doctor go. We stay all night so no harm come to you."

That's how these dangerous criminal lepers responded to an act of kindness. Kindness makes for hope in fellow human beings, hope in God, and hope that if God can change another human being, He can also change me. People today are badly in need of hope . . . therefore an act of kindness can be of great help in making hope come alive.

KINDNESS PAYS OFF

This little six line poem sums up what I've been attempting to say:

I have wept in the night
    For the shortness of sight
That to somebody's need I was blind.
    But I never have yet
Felt a twinge of regret
    For being a little too kind.
                    Author unknown

Let's apply the laws of kindness to such a simple thing as gossiping. Before you hear any tidbit of gossip ask yourself these questions: Is it true? Is it necessary? Is it kind? That's how kindness is translated into a practical application.

Kindness is always a source of good will. Companies and organizations spend millions on the creation of good will. But a single act of ill-will or an act of injustice can set the process back. Most retail outlets work on the premise that the "customer is always right," and needs to be treated with honor and respect. Should our homes and our churches treat people with any less emphasis on kindness?

The biblical word for kindness is from the Greek word *chresteuomai,* which means "to show oneself useful, to act benevolently." Therefore, in order to experience the pay-off of kindness, it must be first acted out by someone. It's much more than an attitude . . . it's an action interpreted by the recipient as an act of kindness. It's an act done with a pure motive. It's something that is useful to another.

Jesus has a way of cutting away all peripherals to get to the point. Listen: "But love your enemies, do good, and lend, hoping for nothing in return; and your reward will be great, and you will be sons (daughters) of the Most High. For He is kind to the unthankful and evil. Therefore be merciful, just as your Father is merciful" (Luke 6:35-26;NKJV).

Do you want to be identified as a son or daughter of God? As you do good and as you share deeds of kindness the promise is that you will be children of the Most High. Why? Because God is kind. You take on the very character of God as you unselfishly share deeds of kindness with others.

KINDNESS IS GOD'S WILL

In case you're thinking that kindness is an optional choice in human relations, take a look at the command, "And be kind to one another, tenderhearted, forgiving one another, even as God in Christ forgave you!" (Eph. 4:32;NKJV).

I remember an act of kindness I witnessed as a young boy. My father and I were driving down a snowy street in Mansfield, Ohio when we came upon a car stuck in the snow. Dad stopped our 1940 Pontiac and got out to help free the other car. It happened to be driven by a black man, and his family was in the car with him. My dad and the black man worked side by side to move the car.

When the family was ready to go down the street, my father pulled off his warm, fur-lined gloves and gave them to the man who had none. I watched as the other man got in his car, with a tear on his cheek. I waved happily as they went down the street. I don't know what that act of kindness did for that other family, but I know that's been a positive influence in my own life. It's an object lesson that lived on.

Kindness has a fantastic pay-off . . . to the person who is on the receiving end and also the person who performs the act of kindness. Kindness is a quality of life that cannot be replicated by technology.

The following anecdote is related by Rebecca Pippert:

> When I first came to Portland, Oregon, I met a student on one of the campuses where I worked. He was brilliant and looked like he was always pondering the esoteric. His hair was always messy, and in the entire time I knew him, I never once saw him wear a pair of shoes. Rain, sleet, or snow, Bill was always barefoot. While he was attending college, he had become a Christian. At this time, a well-dressed, middle-class church across the street from the campus wanted to develop more of a ministry to the students. The congregation was not sure how to go about it, but they tried to make the students feel welcome. One day, Bill decided to worship there. He walked into this church, wearing his blue jeans, tee shirt, and, of course, no shoes. People looked a bit uncomfortable, but not one said anything to him. Bill began walking down the aisle looking for a seat. The church was quite crowded that Sunday, so as he got down to the front pew and realized that there were no seats, he just squatted on the carpet . . . perfectly acceptable behavior at the college

fellowship, but perhaps unnerving for a church congregation. The tension in the air became so thick one could slice it.

Just then, an elderly man began walking down the aisle toward the boy. Was he going to scold Bill? My friends who saw him approaching thought, "You can't blame him. He'd never guess Bill is a Christian. And his world is too distant from Bill's to understand. You can't blame him for what he's going to do."

As the man kept walking slowly down the aisle, the church became utterly silent. All eyes were focused on him; you could not hear anyone breathe. The man reached Bill, and with some difficulty he lowered himself and sat down next to him on the carpet. He and Bill worshipped together on the floor that Sunday. I was told there was not a dry eye in the congregation.[1]

An act of kindness by one man made a difference in this young believer's life. Kindness is an act of the will, resulting in a glimpse of God's love by the person on the receiving end of the act. There's no doubt about it — kindness makes a difference in life!

Love is . . . KIND!

3

Love . . . Searches for the Truth

The tremendous power of truth is illustrated by Dr. Paul Brand, a missionary surgeon, who writes:

> I think back to an encounter with trust I had many years ago. Before I trained for surgery, I worked in the general practice of my father-in-law, near London. One day a woman came in with a list of complaints that exactly described gastritis. After a brief examination I told her my diagnosis, but she

looked up at me with large, fear-filled eyes.

I repeated to her soothingly, "Really, it's not a serious condition. Millions of people have it, and with medication and care, you'll be fine." The fear did not leave her face. Lines of tension were etched there as if I had said, "Your disease is terminal."

She quizzed me on every point, and I assured her I would be doing further tests to verify my diagnosis. She repeated to me all her symptoms and kept asking, "Are you sure? Are you sure?" So I ordered a barium meal and extensive x-rays.

When the test results came back, all pointed conclusively to gastritis. I saw the woman on one last visit. She trembled slightly as I spoke to her, and I used my most comforting and authoritative doctor's tone. "It is perfectly clear . . . no doubt . . . that you have gastritis. I thought so from the first visit, and now these tests have confirmed it. The condition is chronic and will require you to change diet and medication, but it should settle down. There is absolutely no reason for alarm."

The woman stared into my eyes with a piercing gaze for at least a minute, as if she was trying to see into my soul. I managed to hold her gaze, fearing that if I looked away she would doubt me. Finally, she sighed deeply, and for the first time her face relaxed. She sucked her breath in sharply and said, "Well, thank you. I was sure I had cancer. I had to hear the diagnosis from somebody I could trust, and I think I can trust you."

She then told me a story about her mother, who had suffered through a long, painful disease. "One tortuous night the family doctor made a house call while mother was groaning and pressing her hands to her stomach. She was feverish and obviously suffering. When the doctor arrived mother said, 'Doctor, am I really going to get better? I feel so ill and have lost so much weight . . . I think I must be dying.'

"The doctor put his hand on my mother's shoulder, looked at her with a tender expression, and replied, 'I know how you feel. It hurts badly, doesn't it? But we can lick this one . . . it is simply gastritis. If you take this medicine for a little while longer, with these tranquilizers, we will have you on your feet in no time. You'll feel better before you know it. Don't worry. Just trust me.' My mother smiled and thanked him. I was overwhelmed by the doctor's kindness.

"In the hallway, out of her hearing, the doctor turned to me and said gravely, 'I'm afraid your mother will not last more than a day or two. She has an advanced case of cancer of the stomach. If we keep her tranquilized, she will probably pass away peacefully. If there's anyone you should notify . . . .'

"I interrupted him in mid-sentence, 'But, doctor! You told her she was doing fine!'"

This woman, now a middle-aged patient herself, had first gone to that same family doctor with her stomach pains. He had put a hand on her shoulder and said gently, "Don't worry. It's only gastritis. Just take this medicine, and you'll be feeling fine very soon." And he smiled the same paternal smile he had shown her mother. She had fled from his office in tears and would never see him again.[1]

Truth is a rare commodity in today's world. Truth lies trampled in the streets under such things as expediency, getting ahead, just this once won't matter, no one cares, and in the name of doing your own thing. It's so rare that when a person is honest enough to return a purse or billfold to its rightful owner it may make headline news in the local paper. Truth is the actual state of reality, it's a fact. Why then is it so elusive?

SEARCHING FOR TRUTH

Many times the truth is hidden because it's too painful to deal with. We as human beings don't like the truth when it hurts. If love is to be a seeker of the truth it doesn't settle for the obvious. To search for truth is to dig for it . . . not be satisfied with easy, simple answers. Love searches to uncover the real story.

Dr. Richard Selzer, a surgeon at the University of Dallas Medical School, has been called a "craftsman with pen and scalpel." He spoke of searching "for meaning in the ritual of surgery, which is at once murderous, painful, healing, and full of love."

In his book, *Letters to a Young Doctor*, Dr. Selzer writes about accompanying a doctor to Honduras during his residency. A young girl came to them with a cleft palate, a deformity of the lip so grotesque she would not remove from her face the cloth that shielded her imperfection.

During surgery the young girl died, an unforeseen reaction to the anesthetic. At the funeral, the girl's mother greeted Selzer with profuse thanks, for her daughter had gone to heaven with the resurrected beauty for which she had prayed. The young doctor, Selzer realized, had slipped into the hospital morgue at night and completed his surgery. An act of vanity and denial, Selzer thought at first. But in the retelling of the story, over a decade later, Selzer sees the doctor differently. "I would like to have told him what I know now, that his unrealistic act was one of goodness, one of those persevering acts done, perhaps, to ward off madness."

The unending search for the truth is one of those continuing acts to ward off madness. Without truth, there can be no meaningful human relationships. Without truth, our society breaks down. Without truth family life cannot be nurtured.

THE FOUNDATION OF TRUTH

In what Bonhoeffer calls this time "in-between" the creation and the final resurrection, we ward off madness with persevering acts of truth seeking. We find reason for going on in the truth of His life, death, and resurrection in victory! Religion cannot exist, a personal relationship with God cannot be possible without the truth being a vital foundation upon which to build. The bedrock of truth is the Bible, God's Word expressed in written form for mankind for all times and all seasons. "God is a Spirit: and they that worship him must worship him in spirit and in truth" (John 4:24;KJV).

The Bible states simply, "God is love" which can also be transliterated as "God is truth." He is the great I AM. He exists and I must believe that! He is the ultimate truth. Having begun with this basic, it's easier to find truth in human relationships.

Consider this modern parable about a young mother who went to see a psychiatrist: The doctor had established that she was a wife and mother of three children and almost at random he asked, "Which of your three children do you love the most?"

She answered instantly, "I love all three of my children the same."

He paused. The answer was almost too quick, too glib. He decided to probe a bit. "Come, now. You love all three of your children the same?"

"Yes, that's right," she said. "I love all of them the same."

He said, "Come off it now! It is psychologically impossible for anyone to regard any three human beings exactly the same. If you're not willing to level with me, we'll have to terminate this session."

With this the young woman broke down, cried a bit, and said, "All right, I do not love all three of my children the same. When one of my three children is sick, I love that child more. When one of my three children is in pain or lost, I love that child more. When one of my children is confused, I love that child more. And when one of my children is bad . . . I don't mean naughty, I mean really bad . . . I love that child more." She paused, then she added, "But, except for those exceptions I do love all three of my children the same."[2]

We serve a God who knows and loves us just the same as He knows and loves all other human beings on this planet. That's bedrock truth! And that's the truth about real family and human relationships. When people are hurting, God is there in love. We need to be there in love, in truth, when others around us are hurting. This can be personalized truth. The early church father Augustine said, "God loves each one of us as if there were only one of us to love."

And there are times when truth is more than a solitary search by one person. There are moments when this search for truth is a collective search, a time of people coming together to mutually find the truth.

Once a Jewish Chassidic teacher told this parable: A man had been wandering about in a forest for several days, unable to find the way out. Finally, he saw a man approaching him in the distance. His heart was filled with joy. *Now I shall surely find my way out of this forest,* he thought to himself. When they neared each other, he asked the man, "Brother, will you please tell me the way out of the forest? I have been wandering about in here for several days and I am unable to find my way out."

Said the other to him, "Brother, I do not know the way out either, for I too have been wandering about in here for many days. But this much I can tell you. Do not go the way I have gone, for I know that it is not the way. Now come, let us search for the way out together."[3]

In love's unending search for the truth there will be times when the truth can best be found in cooperation with other searching people. If we join our hearts and hands in the walk of love and search for truth collectively as the body of Christ we can find our way in this life. Life within the Church is a cooperative effort. Everyone of us is important and has something to contribute to make the whole body complete. I believe the same application can be made in the discovery of truth. It has been said that two heads are better than one — the best application may be in the search for truth.

DEADLY DANGER OF LIES

Why is it necessary to search for truth? The truth is

not so popular as gossip or innuendo. Too often truth is hidden by others on purpose. In the second or third telling of a story it has become embellished by untruth. Love must consider the source and keep at the task until the real facts are uncovered.

Why is it necessary to keep on searching for truth? There are some people who would rather share the non-truth or the exaggerated truth. There are some who love to jump to conclusions, who build a case on hearsay, who desire to put others down so they will look better themselves.

Why is the search for truth necessary? The truth may just save someone's life.

This is illustrated in a story of how gossip — lies — can kill. The victim was a girl named Gloria, the teenage daughter of a prominent citizen in the town. Gloria had been seen, according to the gossip, getting out of a young man's car at seven in the morning. Tongues began to wag. It was reported that her evening dress was rumpled. She was said to have staggered up the steps to her home. The gossip made the rounds, growing in detail as it went. There was talk of a wild weekend house party at a nearby college. The gossips of the community drew their conclusions and treated Gloria accordingly. Everywhere she met with stares and si-lence of huddled whispers. A few weeks later Gloria, her heart broken, wrote in her diary: "I am not what they say. I would rather die."

Then she took an overdose of sleeping pills and got her wish. But it wasn't the end for that community. The subsequent police investigation brought out the truth. Gloria had gone to a college dance with several other girls. They had missed the last bus home. With their parents' knowledge all had spent the night in a women's dormitory at the school. The father of one of the girls had gone for them early the next morning and taken each of them home. Gloria had staggered because of weariness, not drink or drugs. The young man in the car and Gloria's disheveled clothing were the creations of an imaginative and talkative woman, who had seen the girl's arrival and found it a juicy morsel for her morning round of phone chats. When the investigation was finished, the town felt terrible. But it was too late. Gloria was dead.[4]

Truth brings life . . . untruth brings death! Perhaps that's why Jesus said, "And you shall know the truth, and the truth shall make you free" (John 8:32;NKJV). Truth will set everybody free! The truth will set you free from the consequences of the lie. One of the most endearing components of this thing called love is the undying desire to get to the truth, especially in human relations. It's not an easy task, but it can bring freedom to others as well as ourselves.

Let's take a look at one more life-application of this facet of love: A man returned to work in a business where he had been fired several months previously. This time his work was superior. His supervisor, remembering how inconsistent he had been in the past, asked, "What happened to make such a difference in you?"

The returned employee told this story:

When I was in college I was part of a fraternity initiation committee. We placed the new members in the middle of a long stretch of a country road. I was to drive my car at as great a speed as possible straight at them. The challenge was for them to stand firm until a signal was given to jump out of the way. It was a dark night. I had reached one hundred miles an hour and saw their looks of terror in the headlights. The signal was given and everyone jumped clear . . . except one boy.

I left college after that. I later married and had two children. The look on that boy's face as I passed over him at a hundred miles an hour stayed in my mind all the time. I became hopelessly inconsistent, moody, and finally became a problem drinker. My wife had to work to bring in the only income we had.

I was drinking at home one morning when someone rang the doorbell. I opened the door to find myself facing a woman who seemed strangely familiar. She sat down in our living room and told me she was the mother of the boy I had killed years before. She said that she had hated me and spent agonizing nights rehearsing ways to get revenge. I then listened as she told me of the love and forgiveness that had come when she gave her heart to Christ.

She said, "I have come to let you know that I forgive you and I want you to forgive me."

I looked into her eyes that morning and I saw deep in her eyes the permission to be the kind of man I might have been had I never killed that boy. That forgiveness changed my whole life.

In this case, the truth of forgiveness and the truth of love in action set a man free to become all that he was meant to be in God's plan. Are there people who need you to search for the truth on their behalf? Your search for the truth on their behalf may be the last piece of the puzzle to make their life meaningful.

Love . . . SEARCHES FOR TRUTH!

4

Love . . . Holds Up under Pressure

The doctor looks up from his chart and over his glasses, "Have you been under a lot of pressure lately?" For the last forty-five minutes or so, the doctor has been probing, exploring, checking, and asking where it hurts. This may now be your first real clue that all is not right.

Shooting pains in your chest or an acute pain in the stomach region may have precipitated this visit. Pressure, stress, burn-out, build-up, pent-up emotion, tension, and anxiety are terms that all of us are too familiar with in today's pressure-cooker kind of world.

The real challenge is not eliminating the pressures of life completely. Our challenge is in putting pressure into proper perspective. We must learn to handle the daily cares of life so they are not destructive. We can eliminate some, but we are not able to live without pressures. We would be like the fish deep in the ocean, accustomed to living under tremendous pressure. When these fish are brought into shallow water, they literally explode due to lack of pressure.

Pressures are caused by the daily demands of life. Home life, job strain, peer pressures, financial needs, retirement, new children — all these and more can bring about pressure in life. So we humbly conclude that the pressures of life are inescapable. Our problem is how to handle life's pressures.

LIFE IS STRESSFUL

It seems that three very timid women from Nashville ventured to New York City for a vacation in spite of the risk of muggings they so greatly feared. Sure enough, into their hotel elevator a rather large black man entered and when the doors closed, he commanded, "Sit down!"

These three ladies immediately squatted on the floor, but nothing else happened until the elevator stopped at the lobby and the man got out. I'd venture to say that these three ladies felt some pressure!

That night a dozen red roses awaited them in their room. A card explained, "Please accept these flowers and my apology. You must not have seen my dog when I told it to 'sit.' I was embarrassed and did not know what to do, so I just got off. I'm sorry." The card was signed, "Reggie Jackson." (For the non-baseball fan, Jackson formerly played outfield for the New York Yankees.)

There was a day and time when life moved at a much slower pace and it wasn't necessary for us to seek a way to avoid it or take medication to handle it. Pressure is a disease of our civilized, modern world. Yet, many among us have come to live with, accept, or adapt to stress in such a way as to no longer be aware of it or its effects on us.

The term "stress" is borrowed from the field of physics or engineering where it has a precise meaning: "The application of sufficient force to an object or system to distort or deform it." We tend to think only in terms of stress being applied to us from the outside; but pressures can erupt from the inside as well. Events do not in themselves, usually, produce stress reactions. It is primarily our perceptions of or reactions to events that make them stressful.

Paul Harvey, in one of his newscasts, related the following:

An elderly lady was sedately tooling her luxury car downtown in Liberal, Kansas. She spotted a parking place that would accommodate her car and carefully aligned herself to back into the slot using the proper method to parallel park. As she put her car into reverse, a young man in a small, red sports car pulled headfirst into her space, parking before she had the opportunity. She rolled down her window and yelled, "Why did you do that, young man?"

To which he flippantly replied, "Because I'm young and quick." Then made a dash through the front door of the store.

In a few minutes he returned to find

this little lady in her huge luxury car driving ahead and then backing into the side of that little sports car. Forward and — slam — back! Over and over again she did this. The little red sports car was demolished.

He ran to her car door, demanded she roll down her window, and shouted at her, "Why did you do that?"

To which she sweetly replied, "Because I'm old and rich!"

That's one way of handling stress, but not recommended, unless you have deep pockets and are not concerned about traffic tickets!

HOW MUCH IS TOO MUCH?

You probably will acknowledge a moderate level of stress is almost a necessity in order to be productive in our day. Consider that in order for music to be played on a piano, violin, guitar, or cello there must be tension on the strings. But too much will put it out of tune or even break the string.

The fact that disease can be brought on by pressure has been quite well documented by Doctors Holmes and Rahe of the University of Washington Medical School. They devised an inventory of 43 life-changing events that have proven to be powerful distressers and then assigned each of these a score. Without giving you the entire chart, let me illustrate a few of these:

#1 is the death of a spouse which is scored at 100 points
#2 is a divorce — 73 points
#6 is a severe personal injury — 53 points

#20 is when you take out a mortgage of more than
$10,000 — 31 points
#23 is a son or daughter leaving home — 29 points
#41 is a vacation — 13 points

Early research, which has been backed up by further study, shows that a person with a score of less than 150 has a 37 percent chance of becoming ill in the two years following a year that accumulated 150 points of stress. A score of 150 but less than 300 rates a 51 percent chance of incurring an illness following such a stress filled year. A score in excess of 300 within one year, means the chances are 8 in 10 that you will develop a debilitating illness over the following 24 months. This relationship between mind and body is intriguing. But the correlation is well established.

> *Consider that in order for music to be played on a piano, violin, guitar, or cello there must be tension on the strings. But too much will put it out of tune or even break the string.*

During the siege of Stalingrad during World War II, the citizens were subjected to three years of bloodshed, brutality, and near starvation. While the fate of this city hung in the balance for these 36 months, the proportion of people with high blood pressure rose from 4 percent to 64 percent. For the most part the affected persons continued to manifest a hypertensive pattern even after the eventual Nazi defeat. Follow-up studies have shown that they, as a group, did not reach their normal life expectancies. Life was shortened by an average of ten years because of increased pressure.

Previous to the 1920s, heart disease was almost unheard of. Today, more Americans die from heart-related diseases than from any other single cause. We are well aware of the effects that pressure has on us physically, mentally, socially, and spiritually. Is there some hope? Yes . . . the answer to stress is: Love.

LOVE BEARS UP UNDER PRESSURE

That's some hope and help! Love is one of the strongest of all antidotes in the battle for normalcy.

One man whose writings offer some help apparently experienced much the same sense of being pressured as we do. Listen: "Besides everything else, I face daily the pressure . . ." (2 Cor. 11:28). This could easily be written by you or me today, but it was the confession of St. Paul nearly two thousand years ago. When you feel overwhelmed by life, read that entire Bible chapter. It's also a good dose of reality for self-pity.

The squeezing of life goes on all the time. Yet here's the command: "Don't let the world around you squeeze you into its own mold, but let God remake you so that your whole attitude of mind is changed!" (Rom. 12:2;Phillips). We are to resist and let God! Say it with me, out loud: "Resist the pressure and let God!" Let God remake you! Remake you with what? With His generous dose of love! Love on the inside will help you resist the pressures of life on the outside. I believe we have overlooked this thing called "love" as a powerful weapon in our arsenal against stress.

A number of years ago, when the great "Forth Bridge" in Scotland was nearing completion, the contractors tried unsuccessfully to bring the main girders together so they could be bolted and welded. It was impossible. They tried every available device of mechanical power at their disposal. They applied pressure, they pushed and pulled, but to no avail. It just refused to come together. At the day's end, they were completely baffled. They checked out blueprints. They called suppliers. It was supposed to fit but just didn't. One detail that must not be overlooked: the day was cold, cloudy, and overcast.

The next morning, the sun shone brightly, without a cloud to obstruct the warmth on those great masses of steel. The expansion in the girders produced by the heat soon enabled the connections to be made.

In the same way, the love of God flowing in and through us works irresistibly in the silent influences of love more than in any other kind of manifestation. As we have been warmed and influenced by the love of God, we can better withstand the pressures of life and therefore in turn we can offer this same kind of help in manifested love to others who are also under pressures.

Let's be more specific. In order to illustrate from life, let's take a look at Job. I took some time to calculate how Job fared on the "Social Readjustment Rating Scale" of Doctors Holmes and Rahe. The background reading is from the book named after him, Job 1:13-19. Let's chart the changes; and as we do, remember all this pressure came upon him in a single day.

In one day Job experienced a change in financial status, 38 points (vs. 14); another financial change, 38 points (vs. 16); and another in verse 17 for a total of 114 points due to financial change. Verse 19 records the news of the death of ten family members, at 63 points per each death, he scores 630 points. Add this up for 744 points in one day. But that's not all. We can add another 53 points for personal illness (Job 2:7) and another 35 points for arguments with his spouse and he's at 832 points. Talk about a prime candidate for a nervous breakdown!

But Job did not break down or fall apart. Let's look at how Job handled his pressure.

Job let his grief ventilate. "At this, Job got up and tore his robe and shaved his head" (Job 1:20). Very acceptable for his day. Now if you shave your head in grief today, that may not be acceptable . . . but the principle is still the same. Too many of us tend to keep it all bottled up inside. Job expressed his grief. It's okay for real men to cry, too. Hiding from the fact that we are frail and hurt will not help. When we let it all out, there is a therapy of healing already in progress. It's a wound that can heal clean.

Job worshipped. "Then he fell to the ground in worship" (Job 1:2). In worship our perspective is changed. David is an example of one who constantly took his cares and worries to God in worship. Read through the Psalms, but read between the lines. The pressures were often more than he was able to bear, but David found that God was in the midst of his problems. One phrase allows us to catch the concept: "God is our refuge and strength, an ever-present help in trouble!" (Ps. 46:1).

Job did not sin. Now this is important. It speaks of spiritual discipline. "In all this, Job did not sin" (Job 1:22). One thing that is too easy to do when pressured by life is to curse God, curse our life, go our own way. And when under the stresses of life it is easy to sin. Some of the normal restraints tend to disappear in the heat of the pressure-cooker. This was an important key . . . Job didn't compound his problems by sinning and therefore separating himself from God.

Job didn't sin with his mouth. This may seem

redundant after the previous concept . . . but the Holy Spirit must have thought it important enough to have recorded it twice for us. "In all this, Job did not sin in what he said" (Job 2:10). Sinning with the mouth and letting it ventilate are two different things. It's not the events of pressure in and of themselves that may give us cause to sin or produce more stress, it's our *perceptions* of the events and our reactions. Life has been described as being composed of 10 percent of the things which happen to us and 90 percent of our reactions to the things that happen to us.

Job talked it through, thoroughly. Job's friends came to be with him, but they all sat together in silence for seven days. What do other people need when in deep distress? Right here may be a key: performed in love, to simply sit, to just be there when it hurts. Neither Job nor his friends had the spiritual insight into what was happening, but they thoroughly discussed it. You need to read the meat of this book to find the discussions . . . no conclusions, but lots of talk and speculation. For the human being, this may not be all bad when under pressure.

Job begins to praise God. Moving on through this litany of pain and misunderstanding eventually brings Job to the place where he again can praise the Lord. There is a difference between worship and praise. Worship has taken place earlier (Job 1:20) but now praise begins to break forth. Read chapters 38 through 42. Praise is very closely related to thanksgiving. "Give thanks in all circumstances, for this is God's will for you in Christ Jesus" (1 Thes. 5:18). There is a therapy of cleansing and rejoicing which helps with life pressures.

The epilogue tells us that Job made it. "And the Lord accepted Job's prayer" (Job 42:9). But let's not stop there. Move on to the next verse for a real key in the ministry of love to hurting people as well as help and healing for your own person. "After Job had prayed for his friends, the Lord made him prosperous again" (Job 42:10). Not all of life's stories have a happy ending. But for the child of God, life is more than just existing down here. At death we enter an eternal existence, where love is the core of living with God in eternity. The Bible simply tells that God **is** love and where God is, love is also present.

There was a party of botanists who were exploring some of the more inaccessible regions of the Swiss Alps in search of new flowers. One day, through a field-glass, they spotted a flower of rare beauty, one that had not previously been catalogued. It lay in a place where it could only be reached by someone being lowered down into a deep ravine by rope. A Swiss lad, watching this activity, was approached by one of the botanists, and offered a sum of money if he would allow himself to be lowered into the ravine to get the flower and then be pulled back up again.

He took one more look at the dizzy depths and said, "Wait, I'll be back soon," and took off over the mountains.

After a while he returned with an older man. He approached the botanist and said, "I'll be glad to go over the cliff now and get the flower if you let this man hold onto the rope. He's my dad!"

To survive the pressures of life, it makes a big difference who holds the rope. It's a long rope of hope that reaches into heaven itself, where we can almost hear a loving Heavenly Father whisper, "Never will I leave you; never will I forsake you" (Heb. 13:5;NIV).

Love . . . HOLDS UP UNDER PRESSURE!

5

Love . . . Always Believes the Best

In the country church of a small village an altar boy serving the priest at Sunday mass accidentally dropped the cruet of wine. The village priest impatiently struck the boy sharply on the cheek. In a gruff voice he shouted, "Leave the altar and don't come back!" That young altar boy became Tito, the Communist leader who ruthlessly wielded his power over Yugoslavia.

In the cathedral of a large city an altar boy serving the bishop at Sunday mass accidentally dropped the cruet of wine. With a warm twinkle in his eyes the bishop gently whispered, "Someday you will be a priest." That young man grew up to become Archbishop Fulton Sheen who influenced many with his love and devotion.

What power there is in a believing, loving, kind word or action. These two incidents were not the only influential people or actions in the lives of Tito or Sheen, but these were pivotal moments that shaped the future of two leaders.

There is a natural human tendency to believe the worst, to put a wrong light on other people. We are curious about tidbits of gossip or scandal and love to uncover dirt about others. Love which believes the best in and about others is the most powerful counterattack to such tendencies. It seems that the more interesting the gossip might be, the more likely it is also to be the untruth. If when we heard the worst about another we kept it to ourselves, that wouldn't be so bad. But there is also the powerful tendency to tell it to others. It isn't the things that go in one ear and out the other that hurt nearly as much as the things that go in one ear, somehow get all mixed up, and then pour out the mouth.

THE POWER OF BELIEF

The power of believing, whether positive or negative, is incredible. Harry Houdini, the world famous escape artist, would issue a standard challenge to each community where he was to perform. He could be locked in any jail cell in the country, he claimed, and would free himself in short order. He always managed to make good on his challenge and promise. But one time something went wrong.

Houdini was ushered into the local county jail in a small community. The heavy metal door slammed shut behind him. Immediately, he took from his belt a concealed piece of metal, strong and flexible, with which to pick the lock from the inside. He set to work immediately. But something seemed to be most unusual about this lock. For thirty minutes he worked and got nowhere. An hour passed and still he had not managed to open the door. He was bathed in sweat, panting in desperation but still was not able to pick the lock.

Finally, after diligently applying all his know-how for more than two hours, Harry Houdini collapsed in frustration and failure against the door he could not unlock. When he fell against the door, it swung open. It had never been locked at all. But it might just as well have been. In his mind he knew it to be locked — that kept him from opening the door and walking out of the jail cell.

By what we believe we keep ourselves locked up. We keep people in cages by what we believe about them. Belief is powerful. *Belief is especially powerful if it is engaged in believing the best!*

There was an elderly lady who had made it a point in her life to never say anything bad about another person, if at all possible. This was the way she lived her life. She refused to accept gossip or believe the gossips about anybody else. She was one of those very positive people who was an influence in her church and community.

This trait of hers was well known. One day she was approached by someone intent on testing her. The question was asked, "There cannot possibly be anything good in the devil, right?"

She considered the questioner, thought a moment, and replied, "Yes, but you must admire the fact that he never gives up."

There is something good to believe about every

person. It's our responsibility to look for it, believe it, encourage it, and express the best.

My mother used to challenge me with these words, "If you can't say anything good about a person, don't say anything."

It's precisely at this point we exhibit our good spiritual breeding. It's here we show whether or not we are part of heaven's gentlewomen or gentlemen.

LISTEN — THEN SPEAK

The writer of that little, sometimes overlooked epistle — James — challenges all of us to develop and live out a belief that behaves gently. The life of Jesus Christ within us should move us toward an action that is putting the best light on others. Here is where Christian living begins to really come to the forefront. Listen: "Everyone should be quick to listen, slow to speak . . ." (James 1:19).

Being "quick to listen" shows a keen interest in others, even being an eager listener, an active listener. What a lost art in our fast-paced world. It seems as though none of us will take the time to listen to those who are hurting. How are we to believe the best about others if we don't have enough interest to share a listening ear? Belief is based on input. That's where it starts . . . this believing the best.

But there's another side of this issue: "slow to speak." We have been created with two ears and one mouth. Perhaps that's more than a subtle hint to listen twice as much as we talk. Yet, we do have one mouth and the mouth is made for speaking. It's more than just creatively listening and believing the best. There must be an action that follows believing. This believing the best must also be expressed by giving word to your believing.

Richard Barthelmess, former Broadway actor, called home to make a date with his lovely wife, Jessica. Theirs was one of those very rare solid homes among the entertainment world. He told her to prepare for an evening to be spent in dinner at her favorite place. He arrived home and the two of them made their way out for the evening. At the restaurant, he had thoughtfully made arrangements for flowers to grace the table, and there was the strolling violinist who stopped at their table to play her favorite song. It was a lovely, romantic, wonderful dinner.

> *We have been created with two ears and one mouth. Perhaps that's more than a subtle hint to listen twice as much as we talk.*

When dinner was finished they drove to their favorite spot overlooking the city, which sparkled in the evening. He took both of her hands in his and looking into her eyes began to tell her how beautiful she was, what a wonderful wife she had been, and how much he loved her. She said, "Richard, I love you, too. This has been a wonderful evening. I know you love me, but why are you doing all of this?"

He looked at her longingly and said, "Jessica, I have just come from the doctor's office. He told me that I have cancer of the throat. Tomorrow surgery has been scheduled which will remove my voice box. This is the last time I will be able to express to you with my voice my deep love and appreciation."

We are so hesitant to tell it, even to the important, meaningful people in our life. Let's not only believe the best . . . let's also tell the best about and to others.

Trust is also closely related to believing the best about others. Think of the kind of world this would be with open, honest, caring, loving trust in the human relationship mix. This would eliminate the haggling at union contract times between management and labor. This would change forever the international strife between nations. With this aspect of love in operation between husband and wife we could put marriage counselors out of business. With trust at work the need for lawyers would all but disappear. Negotiators, arbitrators, peacekeepers would all be out of jobs.

It's at this very point that communication breaks down. We simply do not believe the best; at times, we don't even want to believe the best. We'd rather fight than switch to this kind of attitude which could turn this world on its ear.

BECOMING A POSITIVE BELIEVER

I'm sure you agree that we should move toward this attitude of believing the best . . . but how? Two things may be helpful here.

First, believing is an act of the will, a discipline. We are to disciple our imagination rather than let it run wild. The apostle Paul challenges us to "take captive every thought to make it obedient to Christ" (1 Cor. 10:5). Couple that with the command to think correctly and we have a plan of action. "Whatever is true, whatever is noble, whatever is right, whatever is pure, whatever is lovely, whatever is admirable — if anything is excellent or praiseworthy — think about such things" (Phil. 4:8).

God creates each of us with the capacity to control our thinking. We can't control much else in this world, but we can control our thoughts! This is exactly what is needed as we continue our trek through this life thinking and believing the best about others.

Second, believing in and of itself isn't enough. The challenge is to combine belief with action. "You see that a person is justified by what he does and not by faith (belief) alone" (James 2:24). Believing is an internalized action; no one knows what you are believing — the best or the worst — until it is expressed for someone else to hear. Here again, discipline is involved. It's creating and taking the opportunity to tell it in a language that can be understood.

It seems there was a busy businessman who, if he were honest, would admit to neglecting his wife and family. One day he attended his weekly civic club where the speaker talked about doing something nice for the wife. He said, "When you go home tonight, buy her a dozen red roses. Present them to her, but don't just plop them down — do it with finesse. Then take her into your arms and say, 'These red roses are but a symbol of the deep love and appreciation I have for you. You are the sun in my day, the cream in my coffee, the axle of my wheel; my world revolves around you. I do really love you, dear.'"

This man decided it *was* time to do something special for his wife. He walked into the house with firm resolve to follow through on this beautiful expression. He presented the flowers and said his little speech and gave her a kiss. Her response, however, was not what he expected. She then plopped herself down on the couch and burst into tears.

He was stunned. "Honey, what is wrong?"

Through her sobs she said, "This has been a terrible day. At breakfast, Susie spilled orange juice all over the carpet. Then I got a call from Johnnie's principal to come for a special conference. On the way home the car broke down. When I began washing clothes the washer overflowed. And to top this day off, you have come home drunk!"

Even the best of intentions can be misunderstood, but that should not keep us from translating our believing into an action. "Faith by itself, if it is not accompanied by action, is dead" (James 2:17). Intentions, even if good, mean absolutely nothing if they don't get beyond the action stage. People want more than talk in a relationship, they want action.

Life can be pretty grim. There are setbacks, trials, misunderstandings, troubles, mistakes, problems, and difficult people we are confronted with in our journey through life. What a pleasant and encouraging break in life it would be to have a person in our life circle who is believing the best and expressing the best and hoping the best for our well-being. Think of the outstanding ministry this would be for each of us to have. All of us need an "encourager" in our circle of friends, relatives, or neighbors.

Think of the potential if in some way each of us encouraged one person every day. At least 365 people would be lifted up in some way each year! If you lived only another twenty years after you began this ministry, you would have helped make seventy-three hundred people happier, at least for part of a day.

Consider the heart of Madison Avenue's elaborately engineered system of persuasion at the center of advertising. The single premise is that each group or person in our society has a weakness or emotional need. If it is possible, "Ad Alley" will uncover these psychological problems in surveys and interviews, then target an ad campaign to exploit these discoveries. Jerry Della

Femina, author of *From Those Wonderful Folks Who Gave You Pearl Harbor,* in a interview said, "Advertising deals in open sores . . . Fear. Greed. Anger. Hostility. You name the dwarfs and we play on every one. We play on all the emotions and on all the problems, from not getting ahead . . . to the desire to be one of the crowd. Everyone has a button. If enough people have the same button, you have a successful ad and a successful product."

If there is to be any kind of a move to counter such attitudes, it must come out of a meaningful relationship to Jesus Christ. This, in turn, leads to believing the best of and expressing the best to others.

Love . . . ALWAYS BELIEVES THE BEST!

6

Love . . . Looks to the Future

There is an ancient story which tells about a small village that settled and grew at the base of a mountain. The main source of nourishment was the clear, flowing water from a beautiful mountain stream. This stream had as its source mountain springs high up on the side of the mountain. The stream twisted and turned and bubbled and made its way to the village below. Water from the springs was the source of life for the present and into the future.

There was a hermit who lived high up in the mountain whose purpose in life was to be the keeper of these life-giving springs. His daily duty was to check and clean away any debris, branches, or dirt which in any way might cause the water to be polluted and harm the inhabitants in the village below as they cooked and drank from the stream. Then the hermit became sick, so sick that he was unable to clean out the springs. For weeks he remained in this condition. Gradually debris began to clog the flow and the springs became polluted. The water turned bitter. It became unusable.

In the village it became a cause for alarm. People became sick. Disease began to spread. The village gathered in a town council to search for a solution. Something had to be done and done quickly! In their discussion, one person remembered the hermit whose purpose in life had been to keep the springs clear and clean. A group was then sent to search for him. They found him sick, too ill to keep the springs and the stream clean and clear of debris. The answer was to nurse him back to health again. When healthy, he again became the keeper of the springs and the cool, clean, clear, life giving water flowed once more.[1]

The spring could well represent Jesus Christ as the source of all love and all life. The water, could we liken it to love? Love is the delivery system for the Source. The keeper of the springs? That's you and me! Then the village has to be the people who are a part of your world, especially all those in need of love, those who are fragile, and especially the young.

BUILD A LOVE AWARENESS

How can we keep the springs of our lives clear of debris so love flows freely? First, *let's build a love awareness.* Plato said, "All loves should be simply stepping stones to the love of God. So it was with me; and blessed be His name for his great goodness and mercy."

Our working definition states that "love is an

action directed to another person." Awareness means that we, you and I, need to become sensitized to family members, new neighbors, hurting children, lost youth, friends, and people who do not know Jesus Christ. Reaching out to people with an action that is perceived to be love needs to be a daily agenda for life.

A conscience that is tuned to love-action will not be an automatic happening. The natural, human reaction is to focus within ourselves rather than without to people's needs. Too much of our life style actions are focused on me, mine, myself, and I. Jesus challenged His disciples to simply "look" at the whitened field of opportunity. Look around, become aware. To instill a love consciousness requires continual emphasis. To take the long look when it comes to love is more than a one-time occurrence. Reinforce your love action by the continued looking for the opportunities and people to which it can be focused.

When you have looked until you have become aware of a need, and reacted in love, then reinforce it in your living by rewarding yourself. Tell yourself, "Now that's more like it!" Encourage more love action by appreciating each act of love you see in others as well as in yourself.

Awareness of needs in other persons' lives doesn't always come easy. Some are obvious, but more often than not you need to get to know people before they are willing to reveal needs to you. That may take time; therefore, love is future oriented.

There are many cast members in this play. *Commitment* to others takes some time. *Openness* comes from trusting. *Trusting* comes from listening and spending some time with others. *Loyalty* comes into play with this awareness. *Trustworthiness* is a rare jewel seldom found in human relationships today. This, too, must be part of the mix.

When we refuse to invest the time and effort in any relationship we are sending a signal that in reality we don't care that much. This in turn cuts off the relationship before the love action can even take place. To make love action reality takes some hard work! We must work at maintaining a relationship. We must work at doing these love actions.

> For want of love, a person was lost;
> For want of a person, a family was lost;
> For want of a family, a church was lost;
> For want of a church, a community was lost;
> For want of a community, a city was lost;
> For want of a city, a state was lost;
> For want of a state, a nation was lost.
> For want of love . . .
> *Author unknown*

Bob Kilpatrick emphasizes the importance of individuals with this line from one of his songs: "One by one the world will be won."

MAKE TIME FOR LOVE

We must also structure our priorities so as to maximize love. We make time for all the life activities which we think to be important. If fishing (substitute whatever you want: shopping, golfing, cooking, vacationing, eating, etc.) is a high need in your life, you make the time for it.

The man looked at me and said, "Come on, Pastor, let's be real. My day leaves no time for such activities!" I had just finished speaking about the responsibility that we have as members in the body of Christ to love others, which will take some readjustment of our priorities. He went on: "I'm a realist. Each day I get up at 5:30 a.m., spend about an hour getting to work, work at least ten to twelve hours, then drive back home another hour. I grab a quick bite which will be cold by that time, give my kids a quick good-night kiss and collapse into bed to get ready to do it all over again!" As if that wasn't enough, it seemed I had pushed his button, and he went on, "There is nothing I do, getting to work, working, or coming back home that has the slightest resemblance to what you have said or the Bible teaches." Another pause, this time for the final argument, "Besides, there just isn't time; you're only adding more work and more guilt to my life."

Sure, life is tough and demanding. The urgent always seems to crowd out the really important, the long-term. (I've wondered many times how that argument will go over at the judgment bar of heaven.)

Studies have shown that the average father of today's child will spend less than one minute per day in conversation or touching love. And if he spends that small of an effort showing love to his own child, how much less to those outside his family? Love certainly is not a priority to many in today's get-all-you-can world. What is certain is twenty years from now the job will still be there, but the moments in which to share love actions will have vanished forever.

An excellent place to reset those priorities would be at home, with ones that we live with, ones that we love, people who make up our families. It may mean passing up that promotion requiring out-of-town trips. It may mean your golf score will soar through lack of practice time. Your little ones won't stay little. Don't live with regrets after it's too late to make course corrections.

Our time is just one area love demands. Love intrudes into all corners of life — many we are reluctant to give up.

Much of this dilemma is captured in an old story told by Shalom Aleichem:

> There was this old man standing on a crowded bus hanging on to an overhead strap. The young man standing next to him asked, "What time is it?"
>
> The old man refused to reply. The young man moved on. The old man's friend sensing something was wrong, asked, "Why were you so discourteous to the young man asking for the time?"
>
> The old man answered, "If I had given him the time of day, next he would want to know where I'm going. Then we might talk about our interests. If we did that, he might invite himself to my house for dinner. If he did, he would meet my lovely daughter. If he met her, they would both fall in love. I don't want my daughter marrying someone who can't afford a watch."

Love calls for us to set aside our priorities, our expectations, our desires. As I read the life of Jesus from any of the Gospels, I'm impressed that He took time for the hurting, the disenfranchised. A blind beggar stopped Him,

> *Jesus took time, made time, had the time for people who needed a love action from Him.*

the humble lady with a health problem stopped Him in the middle of an errand of mercy, little children were picked up and touched, lepers got His attention, an outcast woman found Him in conversation over a cup of water, and many more. Jesus took time, made time, had the time for people who needed a love action from Him.

THE NEED FOR LOVE IS CLOSE BY

We can show love by simply taking the opportunities at hand. Just about any person on the street can tell you that all of us are to "love your neighbor" (Luke 10:27). But, who is our neighbor? When Jesus was asked that question He told what we know of today as the story of the "Good Samaritan." What made this man the "good" Samaritan? Let me suggest that he really became the good neighbor because he was aware of human need and took the opportunity offered, and which others had ignored. How about taking the time to read the entire story one more time. (See Luke 10:25-37.)

The apostle Paul, in his letter to the Romans, expressed the same concept in these words, "We who are strong ought to bear with the failings of the weak and not to please ourselves. Each of us should please his neighbor for his good, to build him up. For even Christ did not please himself" (Rom. 15:1-3). Where are the people who are the opportunities for your love action?

The stress scale developed by Doctors Holmes and Rahe (see chapter 5) easily points out who the hurting people can be. They listed forty-three different life events, then ranked them in order of impact beginning with the death of a spouse at 100 points on down to a minor traffic violation at 11 points. Included are such events as a divorce, separation, jail terms, death of a close family member, fired at work, marital reconciliations, retirement, pregnancy, change in health, financial stresses, change to a different job, change in residence, change in school, new mortgage, and even the celebration of holidays such as Christmas. Talk about opportunities for an action of love! Opportunities are everywhere. Simply listen to people at coffee break time. Hear the hurt when people are reaching out for a listening ear. Are you catching on? Wherever you find people you will find people who need love in action.

An opportunity to help may have a very small window through which that love action can be deployed. If we hesitate, the opportunity may be lost.

Did you happen to read the article about Dianne Williams which was carried in newspapers all across the country by the Associated Press? Dianne is a skydiver in her spare time. On this particular day she was attempting to join three others in a midair handholding formation. Unfortunately, she miscalculated her speed and slammed into the backpack of another chutist and was knocked unconscious. This caused her to begin to tumble head over heels like a rag doll as she plummeted toward the ground at a speed between 140 to 160 miles per hour.

Fellow skydiver Gregory Robertson noticed that Dianne was in deep trouble. He straightened into a vertical dive, arms pinned to his body, ankles crossed, head aimed at the ground in what parachutists call a "no life" dive. He was like a dive bomber plummeting towards the ground and Dianne at about 200 miles per hour. At approximately 3,500 feet, about ten seconds before Dianne would hit the ground, Robertson caught up with her. He managed to pull the rip cord on her emergency chute as well as his own chute and they both floated down safely to the ground. His gallant effort was described as "trying to catch a football flopping down the road at 40 miles per hour."

What a rescue! What a story! That's making the most of an opportunity that requires instant action without counting the cost. Think: How many people do you know who are cur-

Are you catching on? Wherever you find people you will find people who need love in action.

rently in a free-fall situation who need to be rescued by an action of love? There is little time to think when an immediate action may be required. This required no small amount of courage.

BE CREATIVE IN LOVE

Sometimes we must create opportunities for love. This is moving into an aggressive stance. More than simply making use of an opportunity offered, let's think in terms of providing the place and creating the possibility of building friendships so that love can be put into action. Here's where the "go" comes in our actions of love. Here is where we will encourage and nurture relationships. Here is where we reach out and invite people to share a meal, take a trip, or share an activity.

From the book *The Friendship Factor* we find a quote by McGinnis: "It is no accident that so many important encounters occurred between Jesus and His friends when they were at the table. There is something almost sacramental about breaking bread with one another."[2]

What's wrong with following this example of the Master? It's basic, and it's been around as long as there have been people and food. The sharing together over a table, whether a full meal or just a cup of coffee, breaks barriers and puts people at ease.

Maybe this would be the point at which to insert a warning about relationships and expressing love. One of the most common problems is that of moving into depth too quickly. The writer of Proverbs states it well: "A righteous man (person) is cautious in friendship" (12:26). There's a time to move slowly which is basic to building lasting, good relationships. Right along with this is the tendency to commit too much too soon. Remember, love takes the long look. You'll have time to let these relationships develop. We'll also do well to remember that many times a love action must be done quickly and must be shared with people who are virtual strangers, which is the other side of the coin.

Love looking to the future is thinking in terms of investment, patience, diligence, and consistency. Right here I'm reminded of the Chinese bamboo tree. The seed is planted in the ground, then watered and fertilized for one year with no growth. The second year, no growth. The third and forth years — no growth. Then, just when you may have forgotten you even planted the seed, the fifth year brings visible results. That bamboo seed will begin to grow, reaching a height of 70 to 80 feet in about six weeks. When did it really begin to grow? When was it important to water and fertilize it? Obviously, from day one with regularity. The continued application of love toward a person or persons may not bear immediate fruit, but with time and patience the results will come.

Commitment is the glue that holds this process together through the ups and downs of any human relationship. There will be times when the energy and time is not available. What then? Do you drop the whole concept? Not if you are committed. Let's go once more to the wisdom of Solomon: "A friend loves at all times, and a brother (or sister) is born for adversity!" (Prov. 17:17). You must not develop relationships only for what you can get from them. And rest assured — your resolve and commitment will be tested.

You may be thinking about now, "I think this may be asking too much of me." It is. But consider that unless love is costly, it is not love. Call it something else, but don't cheapen love actions by discounting the price. Love in action is not a blue light special that has become shopworn and ragged. Love has the dimension of commitment and the long-haul about it. The future will and can be a better place because of the present investment of love today.

Here's how the long-range, looking-to-the-future investment of love pays off, as told by Tony Campolo.

> Miss Thompson was a conscientious teacher who tried to treat all her students the same. There was one little boy, though, who was difficult for even her to like. His name was Teddy Stallard. Teddy didn't seem to be interested in school. He was not an attractive child, his schoolwork was horrendous and his attitude was not better. In short, there was certainly nothing loveable about Teddy Stallard. Indeed, for some strange reason, Miss Thompson felt a great deal of resentment toward Teddy. She almost enjoyed giving him F's. There was something about him that rubbed her the wrong way.

> Miss Thompson knew Teddy's background. His school records indicated that in the first grade he showed some promise but

he had problems at home. In the second grade his mother fell seriously ill and Teddy started falling behind. In the third grade, his mother died. Teddy was tabbed as a slow learner. In the fourth grade, he was far behind. His teacher noted that his father had no interest in Teddy's progress. Miss Thompson knew Teddy's situation, but still there was something about him that she resented.

Christmas time came and the boys and girls in Miss Thompson's room brought her some gifts. To her surprise among those gifts was a very crudely wrapped present from Teddy. Opening it in front of the other children she discovered a gaudy rhinestone bracelet, with half the stones missing, and a bottle of cheap perfume. She put some of the perfume on her wrist which she invited the children to smell. "Isn't this bracelet beautiful?" she asked the children. "Doesn't this perfume smell lovely?" Taking their cue from her, the children responded with appropriate "oohs" and "aahs."

At the end of the school day, little Teddy came to Miss Thompson's desk and said, "Miss Thompson . . . Miss Thompson, you smell like my mother . . . and her bracelet looks real pretty on you, too. I'm glad you like my presents."

When Teddy left, Miss Thompson got down on her knees and asked God for forgiveness for her attitude toward Teddy. To make a long story short, from that day forward Miss Thompson became a new teacher and Teddy Stallard became a new pupil. Both Teddy's attitude and his grades dramatically improved.

Many years later Miss Thompson received a letter from Teddy telling her that he would be graduating from high school second in his class. It was signed, "Love, Teddy Stallard." Four years later she received another letter from Teddy telling her that he was graduating from college first in his class. Four years later there was another letter to inform her that the young fellow who once presented her with a gaudy bracelet with half the rhinestones missing and a cheap bottle of perfume was now Theodore Stallard, M.D. Also, he was getting married. His father was dead now, too. Would Miss Thompson be willing to sit where his mother would sit for the wedding if she were alive? "You are all the family I have left now," wrote Teddy.

Miss Thompson sat proudly where Teddy's mother would have been seated for that wedding. That moment of sensitivity and compassion many years before had earned her that right.[3]

Love . . . LOOKS TO THE FUTURE!

7

Love . . . Is Consistent

A college man walked into a photography studio with a framed picture of his girlfriend. He wanted a duplicate picture made. This involved removing the picture from the frame. In doing this, the studio technician noticed a little inscription on the back of the picture, in a female style of handwriting. This is what it said: "My dearest Walter, I love you with all my heart. I love you more and more each day. I will love you forever and ever. I am yours for all eternity." It was signed, "Cheri," and it also contained this P.S.: "If we ever break up, I want this picture back."

For love to be love, it must be consistent. To be consistent is to be the same no matter the circumstance;

it's a holding firm, it's being fixed, it's something solid which can be counted on. The words that come to mind when thinking about consistency are steady, regular, persistent, unchanging, unified, compatible, and not contradictory. In other words, a love that is consistent can be counted on because it will be there when needed.

"Consistent! No way!" This thought causes chills to crawl up the spines of too many people whose lives thrive on a noncommittal type of living. Today, we want to keep all options open. This philosophy pervades our world-system. No one wants to be consistent unless forced into it by a mortgage or marriage. Such people, even though happy in a current job, will always have a resume or two floating around. While you may value consistency in a relationship, some folks value their options.

The fear of being consistent is epidemic in our Western world. Who wants to be committed? It might be inconvenient, it might intrude on options. We see this trait in college students who are waiting longer and longer before declaring a major. Couples are tentatively entering their marriages with an option of divorce held in reserve as an escape clause. Jobs are accepted with the thought that if this company doesn't appreciate my talents, I still have a few resumes out. Married couples are putting off having children because of the consistency that will be required of them. Personal freedom is valued higher.

Too many relationships are built like the one in which the young man had been transferred to another town, leaving his girlfriend behind. He promised that he would faithfully and consistently write to her, which he did. But at the end of an eighteen month period she got married . . . to the postman who delivered the note daily and in person.

I guess the bottom line, when considering true love in any form, is: Can you be counted on? Will you be there when needed? Will this be consistent? If you cannot commit to being consistent, then let's talk of something other than love.

> Press on.
> Nothing in the world
> Can take the place of persistence.
> Talent will not;
> Nothing is more common
> Than unsuccessful men
> With talent.
> Genius will not;
> Unrewarded genius
> Is almost a proverb.
> Education will not;
> The world is full of
> Educated derelicts.
> Persistence and determination
> Alone are important!
> *Calvin Coolidge*
> *Former U.S. President*

Jonathan Edwards, noted eighteenth-century theologian and preacher, stated his commitment like this:

> Resolved: To follow God with all my heart.
> Resolved also: Whether others do or not, I will!

One of the foundational characteristics of God is

His consistency. This trait is developed in Jesus Christ's life and ministry. "Jesus Christ is the same yesterday and today and forever" (Heb. 13:8). Our response to such affirmations is to live in that assurance. To tell another person that you can be counted on, consistently, is to evoke confidence, which in turn will be tested in the crucible of living. Can you come through time after time? That's the one thing that makes Him God. Let's digress just a bit more. There's a promise upon which this is based. "God has said, 'Never will I leave you; never will I forsake you.' So we say with confidence, 'The Lord is my helper; I will not be afraid, What can man do to me?'" (Heb. 13:5-6). When anything can be counted on to be consistent, it builds confidence and freedom from fear. When love is consistent in its application, the person who is on the receiving end has a freedom from fear; they have confidence in life. What a wonderful gift to be able to give to another.

Several years ago in an arms factory in the United States an unusual experiment was conducted. A bottle cork, weighing less than four grams, was suspended by an almost invisible slender silk thread alongside a steel bar weighing a ton. The bar was hung vertically from the same beam by a length of chain.

Both were motionless when the experiment began. Then the cork was set in motion to swing gently against the steel bar. For a long time there was nothing to be seen except its rhythmic, noiseless swinging back and forth, back and forth, back and forth, while the one-ton steel bar remained motionless. Four grams against two thousand pounds.

More minutes went by, then half an hour, then an hour, and more. Under the relentless hammering of the cork, so nearly imperceptibly as to seem like an illusion, the steel bar moved . . . then stopped. Then it seemed to shudder . . . hung quiet, shuddered again.

There was no deviation in the motion of the cork. Steadily, consistently, without hurry, its noiseless assault continued. After more time the steel bar began to settle into the beginning of an orderly pattern of motion, gradually picking up the rhythm of the swing from the cork.

In about another half an hour the cork, its work completed, was cut down; the steel bar on its own was swinging back and forth like a pendulum.

There is an application for us here. When we encounter seemingly immovable people, we tend to give up. But if an almost weightless cork can, by constant, gentle hammering, set something into motion, surely we can make a difference in our consistent application of love.

Let's get down to specifics by exploring three concepts leading to more consistent love actions.

CONSISTENCY REQUIRES PERSONAL DISCIPLINE

I'm a fan of the underdog. I love it when there's an upset. Maybe that's why I love the old story of the turtle and the rabbit. I can just see the wily rabbit running circles around the turtle. The turtle has no style, no flair; he just plods along putting one foot in front of the other. People laugh, but the turtle never stops, never deviates from his goal. You know how the story ends. While the rabbit takes a nap the turtle lumbers across the finish line the winner!

Give me a turtle any day. All the talent and ability in the world are worthless without the personal discipline to put them into action. Consistency without discipline is about as useless as a Cadillac without gas. It may look great but it takes you nowhere! You can decide all you want to about making your commitment to being consistent and it will amount to nothing without a discipline to make it happen.

Simply stated, discipline is the ability to say "no" and mean "no" to what should not be. The flip side is the ability to say "yes" to what is right and ought to be and translate it into an action, consistently! Discipline will focus your efforts in the right direction.

Self-control is the other way of talking about discipline. It's listed as one of the fruits of the Holy Spirit in a Christian's life. "Like a city whose walls are broken down is a man who lacks self-control" (Prov. 25:28). One major mark of maturity in Christian leadership is self-control, which is evident under pressure. (See Titus 1:8.)

The key to developing this self-control is found in Hebrews. It might be familiar, but read it again with me: "Therefore, since we are are surrounded by such a great cloud of witnesses, let us throw off everything that hinders and the sin that so easily entangles, and let us run with perseverance (consistency) the race marked out for us. Let us fix our eyes on Jesus" (Heb. 12:1-2).

> *We must concentrate on the finish line in order to receive the reward, to hear the "well done" of the Master.*

We are to put aside the needless weight we have accumulated in our life. Worry, selfishness, disloyalty, confusion — all the fat that is keeping us from being in our best shape. These "weighty" items in and of themselves may appear small and insignificant, but added together can really slow us down.

In the same way, sin starts out small, but if continued will grow to entangle and choke like a weed. We must also develop perseverance. Remember, we're running a marathon, not a sprint. Consistent training and consistent discipline are the foundational steps. Finally, this verse encourages us to "fix" our eyes on Jesus. There's our goal. There's our focus. We must concentrate on the finish line in order to receive the reward, to hear the "well done" of the Master. To become consistent in my love actions will take discipline.

CONSISTENCY REQUIRES ACCOUNTABILITY

Few people, left to themselves, will naturally do what is right. Yet we all want to be "left alone." "Don't try to tell me what to do!" is our cry. We resist *accountability*.

Let's say you decide to spend time as a big brother or big sister to an underprivileged child. You set aside one afternoon each week to spend with that child who desperately needs your love. Saturday is the day. You make a promise to the child and yourself that you will be there. The first two or three Saturdays work out just fine; but on the fourth Saturday you are facing a dilemma: spend time with the child sharing love as promised or spend the afternoon water skiing with your friends.

Now what do you do? Choose the fun thing or the right thing? Sacrifice time with the child who desperately needs your love, or spend the day on yourself? Making a commitment to the child may not be enough. You need to be accountable to someone who will hold you to your promises. It may be a spouse, a special friend, a peer, or your pastor. Whomever you choose, make sure he or she is someone who is tough enough to tell you when you are about to make a poor choice. Being accountable to a "softie" is no good.

When we are accountable, two things come into consideration: *accountability for a specific action* and *accountability to a specific person or persons*. Be explicit about the action you want to commit to. Is it to show mercy to the elderly? Then set a number of times you will visit a nearby nursing home each month. Is it to show love to your neighbor? Then establish the number of times you will visit the neighbor each week. The key is to be specific; have a measurable goal.

The one to whom you become accountable can also help you with a swift kick to put your decision into action. There are times and actions that are only carried out with urging by somebody else. The "whom" can be a single person or can be a small group. Two are always better than one — friends sharpen friends.

Becoming accountable to another is a great risk. What if we mess up? Now someone else will know! What if we don't come through with what we promised? Now we can no longer sweep it under the rug. Yet the rewards of becoming vulnerable far outweigh any risks incurred. When a love action has been carried out, consistently, think of the fantastic rewards and sense of accomplishment that is yours!

CONSISTENCY IS REALISTIC

It's easy to become over-committed. It happens, especially when there are so many needy people. Then there's the tendency that once we begin, we must take on more and more responsibility.

How do we guard against over-commitment? First, keep in mind that God does not ask for more than we can fulfill. And when we say "yes" to one thing, we are also saying "no" to other activities and obligations.

There are love relationships that need life-long

commitments, such as to a spouse or other family members. And there are some limited-time commitments to other people and to other activities. The life-time commitments will, by their nature, be few and significant. The limited-time commitments will vary with our opportunities to give.

Suppose that you commit yourself to a commitment consuming two hours per day for six days per week. Will you be able to sustain this? It might work okay for a week or so . . . but can you follow up on this week in and week out? It would be much better to set a more attainable goal (such as two hours per day, for one day per week) and find out you can exceed that.

It will also be helpful if you can tie your love action with a biblical mandate, linking your action to the directive from the Word of God.

For example, we read from Proverbs, "He who gives to the poor will lack nothing, but he who closes his eyes to them receives many curses" (28:27). After reading this you may decide to give to the poor of your community through volunteer service. How do you go about doing that? How many hours will you give? Where will you spend your time? All are questions that you must carefully decide as you remember your prior time commitments.

Consistent is always better than over-commitment, which leads to inconsistency and to the disappointment of yourself and your love action recipient. Okay, you're catching the concept.

It was an ancient rabbi who asked his students how they could tell when night had ended and day was on its way back.

"Could it be when you see an animal in the distance and can tell whether it is a sheep or a dog?"

"No," answered the rabbi.

"Could it be when you look at a tree in the distance and can tell whether it is a fig tree or a peach tree?"

"No."

"Well then, when is it?" the students demanded.

"It is when you look on the face of any woman or man and see that she or he is your brother or sister. Because if you cannot do that then no matter what time it is, it is still night."

"Love never fails" is the way it is expressed biblically. And if love is never failing, it will be consistent in love action. And because it is consistent, others will be able to count on love — perhaps through you — when the chips are down. When all the props have been knocked away from the support system, love comes through. It's there in the form of a loving, caring human being exuding the character of Jesus Christ in human flesh.

The true story we are about to share was told at a pastor's conference in Missouri a number of years ago and should have a source to which credit can be given, but the author is unknown.

It was in one of the Nazi death camps, where the Jews were being exterminated. This particular camp was a work camp and as long as a person could work they were allowed to stay out of the gas ovens. In the family of Solomon Rosenberg the first to go were his aged parents who were well into their eighties and very soon broke under the inhumane conditions of long hours, lack of decent food, and miserable hygienic conditions.

Solomon knew that the next to go in his family would probably be their youngest son, David, who was slightly crippled and thus able to work less and less. Each morning the family was separated for their work assignments, and then returned to huddle together in the barracks at night. The father suffered with fear and trembling, wondering whether this might be the day that their youngest son David would be taken. And so each night as he entered the barracks his eyes quickly sought out his little boy David, his oldest son Jacob, and then the mother of his children.

At last the night came that he had feared. As he walked into the barracks he could see none of his family and he became frantic. His eyes searched again for the precious faces of his family and then at last he saw the figure of his oldest son, Jacob, hunched over and weeping. But he still could not see little David or his wife. He hurried to Jacob and said, "Son, tell me it isn't so. Did they take David today?"

"Yes, Papa . . . today they came to take David. They said he could no longer do his work"

"But Mama, where is Mama? She still is strong. Surely they wouldn't take Mama, too?"

Jacob looked at his father through tearful eyes and said, "Papa, Papa. When they came to take David, he was afraid. And he cried. And so Mama said to David, 'Don't cry

David. I will go with you and hold you close.'"

And so the mama went with her boy to the ovens. She held him close so he would not be afraid.[1]

The psalmist David expressed the consistent characteristic of love like this: "Even though I walk through the valley of the shadow of death, I will fear no evil, for you are with me" (Ps. 23:4).

Love . . . IS CONSISTENT!

8

In between the Positive and the Negative

Are you still with me? Let's keep going.

Translating love into action is a tall order. We've just come through seven characteristics of love, all of which need to be put into action. That's a big challenge! The next section of this book will deal with some of the things that love does *not* do.

There's a feeling today that everything about Christianity should be expressed in the positive only . . . forget the negatives. The "Thou shalt nots" of the Old Testament seemingly have a bad connotation; we think they are a hindrance to the freedoms we must have in Jesus Christ and our Christian life style. Yet the Ten Commandments are not the Ten Suggestions — that is made clear by the way they are stated: ten "thou shalt nots."

Why didn't God state them as positives? Could it be that a negative command is *less* limiting than a positive one? Think, "You are free to eat from any tree in the garden; but you must not eat from the tree of knowledge of good and evil" (Gen. 2:16-17) really allows more freedom than a positive command stated like this: "You have to eat from every tree in this garden, starting with the row in the far northeast corner, then working your way through the center, ending up in the southwest tip, and don't miss one, other than the tree of knowledge which is dead center."

"Do not covet" is more freeing than "I the God whom you serve am setting limits on what you can possess. Every person is entitled to only three cows, one car, not more than a double-team of horses, four suits, one three-room house, and three gold pieces of jewelry."

The Ten Commandments were a beginning, a foundation upon which Jesus Christ came to build the positive. Jesus summarized all of the Old Testament law in two positive commands: "Love the Lord your God with all your heart and with all your soul and with all your strength and with all your mind; and love your neighbor as yourself" (Luke 10:27). It's one thing not to be covetous of any material things my neighbor has, and quite another to care for that person like I care for my own person.

Both forces, negative and positive, are in operation when and where love moves into action. Love is such an all encompassing force that it cannot be defined with only the positive side showing.

A number of years ago a man picked up the morning paper and, as was his custom, first turned to the obituary page. To his horror, his own obituary was printed. The newspaper had made a mistake and reported him as dead. The headline over his obituary read: "Dynamite King Dies." The story went on to describe him as a "merchant of death." He was shown as the inventor of dynamite and a man who had amassed a huge fortune from the manufacture of weapons of destruction. He was shocked — not just at reading of his "death," but at seeing how he would be remembered had he died that day. This incident became a pivotal point, turning his life in another direction.

He made a conscious decision that from that time on he would be remembered as a merchant of love and peace rather than destruction. He devoted the remainder of his life to a new cause. A healing power touched his will. Today we remember him, not as the inventor of dynamite and destruction, but as the founder of the Nobel Peace Prize, Alfred Nobel.

Let's take another look at our working definition: **Love is an action directed to another person that is motivated by our relationship to Jesus Christ and is given freely without a personal reward in mind.**

Our look at love is like holding up a diamond to the light to examine its many facets. It has both the positive and the negative about it. The first part of this book has been devoted to the positive facets . . . now we turn our thoughts to the negative to flesh out our complete understanding of love.

Part Two

What Love Is Not and Does Not Do

Definition: Love is an action — **and the lack of other actions** — directed to another person that is motivated by our relationship to Jesus Christ and is given freely — **and withheld out of respect** — without a personal reward in mind.

9

Love . . . Is Not Jealous

There's an old fable out of the east in which the devil once was crossing the desert and met a group of friends who were in the process of tempting a holy hermit. They had unsuccessfully tried seductions of the flesh. They had assailed him with doubts and fears, unsuccessfully. The holy man was unmoved by all attempts. The devil then stepped forward and proclaimed, "Your methods are too crude. Permit me one moment."

Going to the hermit he whispered in his ear, "Have you heard the news? Your brother has just been made the bishop of Alexandria."

According to the fable, a scowl of malignant jealousy clouded the once serene face of the holy hermit.

Jealousy, the green-eyed god from ancient times, is a contemporary emotion still on the prowl. It's the emotion — quite complex — which can make the heart sink and blood boil.

It was Sir Winston Churchill's standing order that when he returned by train from a trip his dog Rufus be brought to the station to meet him. Rufus would be let off his leash to dash to his master and be the first to greet him.

One day, Norman McGowan happened to be standing nearby when this little ritual took place. Rufus ignored his master and leaped all over McGowan instead. Of course, Sir Winston loved Rufus too much to blame him. Instead, he turned to McGowan with a hurt look and quietly asked, "In the future, Norman, I would prefer you to stay in the train until I've said hello."

Where jealousy is evident, love is not. Coping with this monster is more than many of us are able to do. Let's take a closer look at this most damaging of the negative emotions.

First, the definition of jealousy from *Random House College Dictionary* is:

> 1. resentful and envious, as of someone's attainments or of a person because of his attainments, advantages, etc.; jealous of his brother's wealth; jealous of his rich brother.
> 2. fearful of losing another's affection; jealous of his wife.
> 3. troubled by suspicions of fears of rivalry, unfaithfulness, etc., as in love or aims: a jealous husband.
> 4. solicitous or vigilant in maintaining

or guarding something.

    5. Bible, intolerant of unfaithfulness or rivalry: The Lord is a jealous God.

Some of the synonyms by which we identify jealousy are: envy, resentment, covetous, green-eyed, grudging, possessive, suspicious, mistrustful, wary, anxious, concerned, and obsessed with. That's quite a grouping of negative, destructive emotions. No wonder jealousy cancels out the positive of any love action.

Out of Greek history there comes the sad story of a man who accidentally killed himself through jealousy. It seems that his fellow citizens had erected a statue to one of their number who was a celebrated hero, a victor in the public games which are the forerunners of our present day Olympics. So strong was the feeling of jealousy incited in the soul of the rival that he went to the statue every night with chisel and hammer to destroy the monument. I'm sure you can figure out the end. Each night he chiseled away at the base until finally the statue fell from its pedestal, but in the fall it crushed the man overcome with jealousy.

Let's admit it. We have all had feelings of jealousy at one time or another. (Well, maybe there are some people who have never succumbed, but I personally don't know of any.) Our highly competitive culture has taught us to look out for that person who has what we would like to have. We are not content to enjoy with others their success — we must possess it for ourselves.

Another way of looking at jealousy is as a subtle form of anger gone astray. It's a resentment toward others who have achieved what we had wanted to achieve for ourselves. It's a grudging feeling because someone else is enjoying what we are sure we deserve.

It goes beyond simple wants or desires. It too often involves murderous thoughts, bitterness, and malicious plans to get even.

Examples of jealousy can be found everywhere. Singles envy the married . . . the married envy the singles . . . a middle-age couple envies the home another couple has built . . . a teenager envies the car his friend has bought . . . an unhappy husband envies a friend whose marriage is happy . . . a professor envies the promotion his peer received . . . a doctor envies the skill of a fellow surgeon . . . a pastor envies the growth of a fellow pastor's church. And on and on and on.

Check yourself against this list of some of the common characteristics in jealous people:

- Always striving to make the right impression on others
- Placing others under a critical watch
- Frequent complaints about not being given their just rights
- An insatiable desire for material things
- The need for lots of recognition
- A desire to be in control of others or situations
- Very conscious of status and titles
- Finding it almost impossible to compliment anyone else
- Not generous with time or money
- The ability to hold grudges and the tendency to "keep score"
- Enjoying tidbits of gossip, particularly if it's negative, about other more successful people

The Bible contains directives on what to do with jealousy and envy: "Therefore, rid yourselves of all malice and all deceit, hypocrisy, envy, and slander of any kind. Like newborn babies, crave pure spiritual milk, so that by it you may grow up in your salvation, now that you have tasted that the Lord is good" (1

> *Jealousy is sometimes evident when others have gone an extra mile, while we stopped after one.*

Pet. 2:1-2). In other words, we are commanded to *grow up* — become mature. Put aside these emotions. The command is to "rid yourselves of **all**" such negatives. Now the question comes to mind, "How can I get rid of envy, slander, deceit, hypocrisy, and malice?" Notice how they all seem to be related. They have been lumped together by the biblical writer.

How can we get rid of jealousy? Let's tackle this problem in two parts.

THE CAUSES OF JEALOUSY

As with most negative, destructive emotions, jealousy is often triggered by other matters. Jealousy can be a response when we have done a mediocre job while others have worked harder. Jealousy is sometimes evident when others have gone an extra mile, while we stopped after one.

We tend to become jealous of people with whom we identify . . . brothers, sisters, family members, people with the same occupation, people of the same age, and so forth. We somehow feel we are measured against these people, and must perform up to their standards. When we fall short, jealousy is often our reaction.

Other people's successes fuel jealous feelings. "Why did he get the raise when I've been here just as long?" "How come she gets her picture on the cover, and mine is stuck inside?" "Why does the pastor always ask her to sing? Isn't my voice good enough?" These words and others like them are heard all too often, showing that jealousy is epidemic in our society.

We are also plagued with a desire for material things. Envy is triggered by desire for things we don't have. A nice house, the newest car, happiness, nice clothes, exotic vacations — all tempt us to feel sorry for ourselves because we do not possess them. It's a miserable life when driven by greed.

Many of us have formed very definite ideas about status, success, and achievement, and we want our share. We have taught this quickly and well to our young. Children soon understand that boys get status and recognition for athletic ability or social prowess. Girls receive their strokes based on their beauty and personalities. There's a need to prove themselves; this drive, unless curbed, pushes us on through adulthood. Even churches encourage people to find, discover, and use their gifts. There's a craving for recognition: we want something more, we want to be perceived as achievers. When this isn't possible, we become jealous of the people who seemingly have reached this level.

Concerning the local church, Paul points out this interaction of sharing, even in the joy of achievements, like this: "If one part suffers, every part suffers with it; if one part is honored, every part rejoices with it" (1 Cor. 12:26). It is easy to come to the aid of someone who is hurting. But can we rejoice when another is blessed? That's the tougher assignment. When we honestly share in another's victory, we are putting aside personal feelings in favor of true empathy. It's an exhibit of giving and loving, which is the opposite of being jealous.

Jealousy takes all kinds of forms. There may be many more reasons for the appearance of jealousy in human relationships, but no matter how it is triggered, it's not good. It's a destructive emotion that diverts our attention from where it should be placed.

When looking at these reasons for jealousy, I can identify with Paul in his despair: "What a wretched man I am! Who will rescue me from this body of death? Thanks be to God — through Jesus Christ our Lord" (Rom. 7:24-25). There is an answer. We can effect a cure with the help of Jesus Christ. We do not have to be forever chained to this negative action.

CONTROLLING JEALOUSY

We must admit jealousy has no place in the person who is seeking to share an action of love. Further, envy is a destroyer of positive actions and has no place when we want to do God's will. I remind you again, from the love chapter, "Love is patient, love is kind. It **does not envy**" (1 Cor. 13:4). The following are some suggestions to help rid ourselves of the green-eyed monster.

• **Accept yourself:** One of the root causes of jealousy is the unhappiness or lack of contentment with our current situation or status in life. Too often, we mistakenly think that the only way we can accept ourselves is based on higher performance. You may be thinking, "Yes, I could accept myself if I had something more going for me." Accept yourself because God took you from where you were and turned you into something special, through the sacrifice of Jesus Christ. Take a minute and hear once more what God demonstrates with His love toward us: "But God demonstrates his own love for us in this: While we were still sinners, Christ died for us" (Rom. 5:8).

There's not a lot that can be done to change appearances. "Who of you by worrying can add a single hour to his life?" (Mat. 6:27). Trust God your maker — He knows and accepts you just as you are.

• **Keep things in perspective:** What is really important? Not urgent, not nice, not pressing, but what's long-term important? What really counts?

You've probably seen the bumper sticker which proclaims "Whoever has the most toys wins!" Jesus challenged us to think that life is made up of much more than the things which we can acquire.

Paul, in his writing to the young man Timothy, puts it straight: "But godliness with contentment is great gain. For we brought nothing into this world, and we can take nothing out of it. But if we have food and clothing we will be content with that. People who want to get rich fall into temptation and a trap and into many foolish and harmful desires that plunge men into ruin and destruction. For the love of money is the root of all kinds of evil. Some people, eager for money, have wandered from the faith and pierced themselves with many griefs." (See 2 Tim. 6:6-10.) This world is attempting to brainwash all of us into believing that more is better and the most is best. There is so much more peace to be found in contentment in Jesus Christ.

Jesus told us that when we get our priorities straight the rest of the necessary things of life will be taken care of. Once more, listen: "But seek first His kingdom and His righteousness, and all these things will be given to you as well!" (Matt. 6:33).

• **Set realistic goals:** Jealousy begins to go as we establish the right priorities. Yet remember: It's important that your life goals are based on God's Word and your personal conviction. So much of what we see as goal-setting is done to please others. Life is not to be lived in a comparison mode in which there is always a looking over the shoulder. If our life is to be lived in the fear of comparison, you are in bondage.

What would God have us do? How much is enough? Would this goal be pleasing to Him? After all, it's God before whom we will all stand one day to be judged for the deeds done while on this earth. It's not any person that we have to please. The best of goals can be made and set based on our genuine desire to please God.

• **Practice generosity:** So much of jealousy is based on *my* desires, *my* wants, *my* wishes, *my* rights, *my* life, and *my* things! When you replace this attitude with a more positive attitude of generosity and giving you have taken a giant step toward ridding yourself of envy. The only way to true happiness is through an honest act of giving. In an act of giving you will find that it brings happiness to another and the boomerang effect comes back to strike you — you can't avoid it.

Do not limit your generosity to simply money. Think, too, of giving the intangible such as support, a word of praise, expression of appreciations, understanding, and sharing enthusiasm over achievements. Try it and you'll find it works! From the Proverbs we read, "A man finds joy in giving an apt reply — and how good is a timely word!" (15:23).

Jealous people are on a never ending search for the good life, yet discontent is just about guaranteed. Why? Because everything this world has to offer is fleeting and transitory and earthly and temporal. Nothing lasts. What you give away you keep. It's a principle of Christian living. You can take nothing with you out of this world . . . but you can send it on ahead through an act of giving to others; even a cup of cold water given for the right motive will have its reward.

There are four simple steps to overcome jealousy. Try them. They are simple, but not always easy. I have found that when I decide by an action of my will, the strength is given to me by God to carry out the resolution. He will not make the decisions for me, but He will supply the strength to give action to my decisions.

Billions of people were scattered on a great plain before God's throne. Some of the groups near the front talked heatedly . . . not with cringing shame, but with belligerence, with envy, with jealousy, and with bitterness.

"How can God judge us?" said one.

"What does He know about suffering?" snapped a brunette. She jerked back a sleeve to reveal a tattooed number from a concentration camp. "We endured terror, beatings, torture, and death!"

In another group a black man lowered his collar. "What about this?" he demanded, showing an ugly rope burn. "Lynched for no crime but being black! We have suffocated in slave ships, been wrenched from loved ones, toiled 'til death gave release!"

Far across the plain were hundreds of such groups. Each had a complaint against God for the evil and suffering He permitted in His world. How lucky God was to live in heaven where there was no weeping, no fear, no hunger, no hatred, no jealousy, nor envy!

Indeed, what did God know about what man had been forced to endure in this world? "After all, God leads a pretty sheltered life," they said.

So each group sent out a leader, chosen because he

had suffered the most. There was a Jew, a black person, an untouchable from India, an illegitimate person, a victim from Hiroshima, and one from a Siberian slave camp.

In the center of the plain they consulted with each other. At last they were ready to present their case. It was rather simple: Before God would be qualified to be their judge, He must endure what they had endured. Their decision was that God "should be sentenced to live on earth . . . as a man!"

But because He was God, they set certain safe-guards to be sure He could not use His divine powers to help himself:

Let Him be born a Jew.

Let the legitimacy of His birth be doubted, so that none would know who is really His father.

Let Him champion a cause so just, but so radical, that it brings down upon Him the hate, condemnation, and efforts of every major tradition and established religious authority to eliminate Him.

Let Him try to describe what no man has ever seen, tasted, heard, or smelled . . . let Him try to describe God to men.

Let Him be betrayed by His dearest friends.

Let Him be indicted on false charges, tried before a prejudiced jury, and convicted by a cowardly judge.

Let Him see what it is to be terribly alone and completely abandoned by every living thing.

Let Him be tortured and let Him die! Let Him die the most humiliating death . . . with common thieves.

As each leader announced his portion of the sentence, loud murmurs of approval went up from the great throngs of people.

But when the last had finished pronouncing sentence, there was a long silence. No one uttered another word. No one moved. For suddenly, all knew . . . God had already served His sentence![1]

Need help in ridding your life of jealousy? Go to God! There's understanding and help available. You can live above and without jealousy!

Love . . . IS NOT JEALOUS!

10

Love . . . Does Not Boast

Queen Elizabeth, ruler of England for half a century, was infamous for her much boasting. Her favorite courtier, the Earl of Essex, took part in a plot against his political enemies and was sentenced to die. The queen said, "I would save him, but only if he humbles himself and asks me to." No message came and Essex was put to death.

From that time on, Elizabeth's heartbreak affected her health, for she could not forget Essex. One day, as a lady-in-waiting to the queen lay dying, she sent for Queen Elizabeth and confessed that Essex had indeed entrusted her with a message pleading for his life and had given her his ring as proof; but that she wanted

Essex dead and had therefore never delivered the message. For Elizabeth, this knowledge was a wound from which she never recovered. She did little else for the rest of her days but mourn for Essex. Boastfulness, pride, and selfishness were her undoing.[1]

I remind you of our text: "Love is patient, love is kind. It does not envy, *it does not boast, it is not proud*" (1 Cor. 13:4). Boasting and pride are things that will most often block any true expressions of love. Paul put it plainly: "Love . . . does not boast."

Boasting is the speaking about things connected with oneself with exaggeration and pride. It's the expressions of excessive pride or vanity. It's elevating the self above others. It is a showing of superiority. It's a short-circuit in the connections of being on the same level with others around us.

Our world is full of examples: the taunting celebration of an athlete, the posturing of a dictator, the raving of a self-made businessman, the self-righteous sniveling of a religious institution, the boy-bragging-to-girl, and so forth. Boasting can stop a conversation dead in its tracks.

A man invited his boss home for dinner. The boss was blustery, arrogant, dominating, and boastful. The little boy in the family stared at his father's boss for most of the evening but didn't say a word. Finally, the boss noticed the little guy and addressed him, "Why do you keep looking at me like that, son?"

The boy answered, "My daddy says that you are a self-made man."

The boss beamed and proudly admitted that indeed he was a self-made man and right proud of himself and his accomplishments in this world.

The boy then replied, after the boss paused, "Well,

if you are a self-made man, why did you make yourself like that?"

If only the people who are given to boasting could see themselves as others see them. We see pride in all professions and all occupations. We see it in hunters and fishermen. We all want to make ourselves out to be the heroes of our stories. It can be so subtle. But it can also be blatant and obnoxious.

"Hubris" is the excessive pride, arrogance, or boasting. It is not unique to our society. It all began back in the Garden of Eden. All Adam and Eve had to do to stay in paradise was to allow God to be God. That's all! And it was the one thing they would not do. They decided they would rather trust their own resources. The result was predictable . . . they had to leave the garden. They became estranged from God.

This has not been an easy lesson to learn for Adam and Eve or for the twentieth century person who lives in a society which has idealized the "self-made" person. It's an ideal that is held up to our young and old.

> *All Adam and Eve had to do to stay in paradise was to allow God to be God. That's all! And it was the one thing they would not do.*

And to refrain becomes such a battle for all of us. It would seem that the vast majority of human beings have or will succumb at some time to a boast or two.

One day, Michelangelo happened to overhear a group of people admiring his *Pieta*. One man attributed the sculpture to Il Gobbo, much to the chagrin of Michelangelo, who took particular pride in the *Pieta*.

Returning to the sculpture after dark that evening, he carved his name on it, so that no similar mistake could occur in the future. This is believed to be the only time that Michelangelo identified one of his works in this way.[2]

Is there any hope for us? These suggestions may not be profound, but I hope they will give us a handle where we can begin.

RECOGNIZE BOASTING IN YOURSELF

When we see this trait in others it's repulsive — yet we are so reluctant to be honest with ourselves. Admit it! Come clean! Face it! Say it with me, "I admit that I am given to making myself look better than I am. I admit that I am given to boasting. I admit that I am prone to this exhibition of pride and I need help!" There, now, don't you feel just a bit better? Confession is always a good start in ridding ourselves of an unwanted trait.

Yet do not mistake this first step for the only step. Boasting is a deeply-rooted characteristic that takes diligence to remove. Just as a dandelion has roots that run several feet below the ground, so boasting and pride start from deep within.

Boasting can be expressed in many ways, but it always grows from a haughty, superior attitude. Probably the most repugnant is spiritual boasting. This spiritual pride led to the original fall of the angels. Read the story from Isaiah 14: 12-17. In this short passage, we can count five times where Satan says, "I will . . . ." He was expressing it in a boast: "I will ascend above God!" This kind of pride and the boasting which accompanies it are worthy only of the judgment of God. It causes us to trust in our own ability and virtue rather than trusting in God. It's an expression of smugness, self-satisfaction, and conceit. It's the strutting of a bum in filthy rags who has the audacity to think that he may be the best dressed of all people. If this stance were not so tragic, it would be humorous.

C. S. Lewis refers to this as The Great Sin: "There is one vice of which no man in the world is free; which every one in the world loathes when he sees it in someone else; and of which hardly any people except Christians ever imagine that they are guilty themselves . . . . There is no fault which makes a man more unpopular, and no fault which we are more unconscious of in ourselves. And the more we have it ourselves, the more we dislike it in others."

Lewis continues, "It was through pride that the devil became the devil; pride leads to every other vice: it is the complete anti-God state of mind."

Lewis himself admits that that might sound a bit exaggerated, but then again comes back with this, "A proud man is always looking down on things and people; and, of course, as long as you're looking down, you can't see something that's above you . . . . If anyone would like to acquire humility, I can, I think, tell him the first step. The first step is to realize that one is proud. And a biggish step, too. At least, nothing whatever can be done before it. If you think you are not conceited, it means you are very conceited indeed."[3]

Boasting can be because of intellectual pride. There are many who suffer from this delusion as noted by Paul: "We know that we all possess knowledge. Knowledge puffs up, but love builds up. The man who thinks he knows something does not yet know as he ought to know" (1 Cor. 8:1-2). This kind of boasting will show itself in an arrogance toward the uneducated or illiterate or oppressed. It forgets that all mental capacities have been God-given; whatever knowledge we have is the fruit of lots of other people's labors. There is no such things as a self-taught man.

The philosopher Plato was entertaining some friends in a lavishly furnished room. Among the furnishings was an ornate couch. One of his friends came in — dirty as usual — walked over and trampled on the couch saying, "I trample upon the pride of Plato."

Plato mildly answered, "But with greater pride, my friend."

Intellectual boasting is too often the enemy of loving relationships; it gives its possessor a self-confidence rather than a God-confidence. The intellectual boasting that is given to smugness is hated by God. "Do you see a man wise in his own eyes? There is more hope for a fool than for him" (Prov. 26:12).

> *We brought nothing with us into this world and we can carry nothing out of this world. You'll notice that not too many funeral hearses have trailer hitches for a U-haul.*

Another manifestation of boasting is found in the pride of material possessions. In boasting of material things, self is enthroned instead of God. Secondary things are elevated to the first place and we have a life-style which is unbalanced. As a person begins to boast about what they have rather than who they are, the soul shrivels. This lust for more can be as habit forming as any other kind of addiction.

Why all this unjustified pride of material things? Out of the Old Testament comes the reminder from Job that we were naked when we came into this world and we will depart it in the same condition. We brought nothing with us into this world and we can carry nothing out of this world. You'll notice that not too many funeral hearses have trailer hitches for a U-haul.

One more kind of boasting comes from social standing. This may show itself in class, color, or racial arrogance. God doesn't make the kinds of distinctions that people tend to make.

Former House Speaker Tip O'Neill tells about walking into the Denver Airport and being approached by a man who said, "Hi, Tip. How are you?"

O'Neill replied, "Hi. How are you? Nice to see you."

The man look at him quizzically, then said, "You don't know who I am, do you?"

"Well," said the congressman, "my name is Tip O'Neill. I'm six feet, three inches tall, weigh 265 pounds, have a bulbous nose, gray hair, and cabbage ears. Once you see me, you never forget me. But you're different. Why don't you say, 'Hi, I'm so-and so, Tip. I'm delighted to see you.'"

"That's very interesting," said the man, "because I had supper with you last Wednesday night in Washington. And my name is Robert Redford."[4]

The tendency to boast and brag and be proud is so innately human. We need to be hard on this aspect of living. This flesh in which we are housed so desperately wants to be recognized as something special that it's a constant battle we are waging. What can be done about this seemingly terminal condition?

CURE FOR BOASTING

After acknowledging the problem we must move

to confession and humility in the presence of God. We need to see this as the sin which it is. And sin must be dealt with ruthlessly.

Here's the promise upon which to make that confession: "If we confess our sins, he is faithful and just and will forgive us our sins and purify us from all unrighteousness" (1 John 1:9). And that is one huge *if*. "If" means that it is an act of the human will. *If* I will humble myself . . . *if* I will acknowledge that I need help . . . *if* I will recognize the need for change . . . *if* I am honest enough with myself . . . *if* I am honest with God . . . *if* I am really wanting to come clean . . . all important conditions. There is no remedy for the boaster until that person comes the way of acknowledgment and confession. It's a humbling proposition to say, "God, I am a boaster. God, I am proud. God, forgive me!"

"If we confess our sins. . . ." It is not just saying, "Lord, *if* I have sinned by being too proud, help me." It is a confession of our sins . . . specific sins, each time I sin with my mouth, each time I sin by expressing the pride of my life. It's saying, "Lord, yesterday at lunch, I boasted about my latest accomplishment to a captive audience. Please forgive me."

Here's the challenge: "Your attitude should be the same as that of Christ Jesus, who, being in very nature God, did not consider equality with God something to be grasped, but made himself nothing, taking the very nature of a servant" (Phil. 2:5-7). No one will enter the Kingdom proudly. Nobody will be able to walk up to God with a boastful, prideful spirit and be accepted. Nobody!

Samuel Taylor Coleridge wrote: "And the Devil did grin, for his darling sin is pride that apes humility."

PROTECTION FROM BOASTING

It's not only winning the initial victory over boasting and pride that counts. Can you continue to walk without this spirit of boasting? Can you experience successes in life without boasting about them? Can you acquire possessions without boasting about them? It's not a one-time battle. We must daily walk in victory over pride. Then, when you walk in your victory, you will have to watch that boasting over keeping the victory doesn't become your next downfall. We can boast about the fact that we no longer are given to boasting; we can take pride in our humility. What wretched people we can be. Pride is an enemy that requires us to keep a constant, brutal, honest watch on our motives to overcome. And we must watch *our* motives — no one else's.

I cannot vouch for the truth nor the source of this exchange which is supposed to have taken place between Nikita Khrushchev, then Russian leader, and President Kennedy. It was heated and expressed strong opinions. Finally, Kennedy asked Khrushchev, "Do you ever admit a mistake?"

The Soviet Premier responded, "Certainly I do. In a speech before the Twentieth Party of Congress, I admitted all of Stalin's mistakes."

"Love . . . does not boast!" Why? Well, we've just taken a look at a whole host of reasons. The bottom line is that it's sin when boasting is an expression of pride. What a lot of sand this is in the gears of relationships. Real love does not boast, but in humility puts love into an action.

Louis the XIV of France was considered one of the most powerful kings who ever reigned. He is the king who said, "I am the State!" He was call the "Sun King" because of his glittering, lavish reign and lifestyle. He is the king who built Versailles. He was King Louis the XIV and proud of it. But as happens to all of us, he died. Thousands of people came to his funeral to pay their last respects and to see how a king would be remembered. The crowd filled the great cathedral and spilled out into the surrounding square. He lay at rest in a gorgeous casket. In the entire cathedral there were no lights except a lone, majestic candle stick holding one lighted candle beside the casket.

The greats of France and beyond were there. Flowing eulogies were given in his honor. Then it came time for the bishop of Paris, Masillion, to share the service. He strode to the pulpit, reached out, and snuffed the flame of the candle, then spoke just four words from the darkness: "Only God is great!"

Love . . . DOES NOT BOAST!

11

Love . . . Does Not Embarrass Others

The morning edition of the *Pasadena Star News* of July 20, 1985 carried a heart-warming story about a young man with cancer. Here is part of that story:

> Manuel Garcia feared that when he had shaved his head to get rid of the patches of hair left by chemotherapy, "I would feel very self-conscious that everyone would stare at me."

He didn't need to worry.

Before Garcia was released from the Milwaukee Medical Complex after treatment, his best friend and three relatives came into his room with bald, clean-shaven heads. "I woke up and just started laughing," said Garcia. "Then they told me, 'We're here so you won't be alone.' "

When he arrived home, to his delight he found his house and neighborhood were teeming with bald heads . . . all in the name of love for Manuel Garcia, in his fight against cancer. "My oldest boy had beautiful hair," said Garcia of his son who had wanted his head shaved. "Last night he said, 'Daddy, I did it because I love you.' "

"I cut my hair because I've known him for 15 years and I love him like a father," said Dale Wetzel, 26. "It helped me to understand how he felt; it made me feel good inside."

When Garcia had been diagnosed as having cancer, he was extremely depressed. "But I'm ready for anything now," he says. "I feel 100 percent better."

To "embarrass," according to the *Random House College Dictionary,* is "to make uncomfortably self-conscious; cause confusion and shame to; disconcert; abash." Such behavior is not to be named among people who love.

We embarrass others by such actions as bad manners, rudeness, and ill-spoken words. And while we have all caused others to be embarrassed by our own inadvertent actions, our topic is mostly concerned with deliberate actions that embarrass.

This world is beset with problems more dramatic than causing embarrassment to another. Cancer, disabled children, hunger, abuse — all this and more seem to be of greater importance than being careful about causing embarrassment. But I also know that people who rain embarrassment on others soon discover that it's a slow death to any kind of a loving relationship. Soon others whom we love will begin to avoid us in order to avoid embarrassment. Those we cause to feel uncomfortable certainly will not continue to believe we love them. To build lasting, important, significant relationships takes lots of time and trust; why would any of us want to tear that down and destroy what has taken time to build?

There will be many who read these words and brush them aside by thinking, "Such people are much too sensitive." Sensitivity is another way of saying that love in a relationship is a very fragile thing. It can easily be destroyed. If I really love a person, why would I want to embarrass him or her? Perhaps it comes out of lack of respect for that person or for the relationship. Maybe it's a lack of understanding of another's feelings or sensitivities. In other people it can be caused by callousness. Perhaps you may be that person who tries to embarrass others so that they can be brought down to your level. Whatever the reasons, it should not be a part of any kind of relationship which has been established to show the love of God.

GOD DOES NOT EMBARRASS

The Bible is explicit in 1 John 4:8: "Whoever does not love does not know God, because *God is love!*" (italics are mine). When we read from the first book in the Bible we make the discovery that we are created with deliberate design. "So God created man in his own image, in the image of God he created him; male and female he created them" (Gen. 1:27). We have implanted deep inside our human natures the nature and essence of God the Creator; this nature is activated when we love. When we act like our Maker we set in motion the greatest power in this universe — love! Why, then, do we also want to destroy that nature within us, as well as in the person to whom we direct our love actions, by an act or word which causes embarrassment which is so destructive?

In *Unconditional Love*, Pierre Teilhard DeChardin writes: "Someday, after we have mastered the winds, the waves, the tides, and gravity, we will harness for God the energies of love and then for the second time in the history of the world, man will have discovered fire."

That's the positive thing about love. To embarrass is the negative, opposite side of this beautiful action. Love does not deliberately go out of its way to disconcert, fluster, rattle, or confuse another. To embarrass another will send a very mixed signal which may lead to confusion. "Does so-and-so, who professes to love me, really love me? If so, why do they deliberately embarrass me?"

A very attractive, up-and-coming young couple sat in my office. She was crying, wringing a tissue in her hands, daubing at her eyes which were bleeding mascara in black rivulets down her cheeks. He was slouched in his chair, arms crossed, body language shouting that this is really nothing to be concerned about. She finally came to the point. "I really need to know if John (not his real name) truly loves me."

He nodded his head to indicate that he, in fact,

truly loved Jane (not her real name). Then he spoke, "I really, really, really love her. I work long and hard hours to provide for her. Everyday I tell her that I love her. I have never stepped out on her. I have been faithful to her . . . what more could she be asking for?"

More sobs from her, then vehemently, "Yes, you do all of that and more, but you never miss a chance to put me down, to embarrass me, especially in front of our friends. You really don't love me. If you love me, as you say you love me, you would never embarrass me again!"

He slouched lower, mumbled something about her being too sensitive, and indicated it was time to leave.

She fixed her eyes on him and spoke to me: "John has never loved me. I am window dressing in his selfish life. He'll do anything short of striking me to embarrass me so that he looks like the big macho hero he thinks himself to be. I know that all love has been killed, one embarrassing moment by embarrassing moment, until there's nothing left."

Amazingly, this home and marriage were saved. It took lots of behavior modification on his part as well as hers to turn their relationship around, but he was sincere when he finally began to see the hurt from her perspective. Old habits didn't yield quickly, but John did change, Jane made some course corrections, and together they put it back together. It has a happy ending which all broken relationships could experience.

Maybe it's time to stop and think about your relationships. Are there any in which you have made subtle and not so subtle actions to embarrass another? It's time to be honest and come clean. It's time to ask for forgiveness. It's time, or past time, to get back on course. And for whatever reason or motivation, put aside the habit to embarrass the people who most need your loving support. To you it may not be that big a thing because you're dishing it out, but it's not much fun to be receiving it.

You might also want to take a long look within to determine why it is that you want to embarrass another. Does that rise out of your own poor self image? Does it come because you do not know how to handle awkward situations with grace? Is it because you'd rather destroy than to build?

TO EMBARRASS OR NOT TO EMBARRASS — THE CHOICE IS OURS

All right, the case has been stated. Now, how can we change this hurtful behavior? Did it ever occur to you that you have a choice to make? We have been created with a free will — we choose to build up or tear down. Maybe you feel trapped in this behavior pattern and don't know how to change. Choice is the place to start. Think of this not so much as a problem, but rather an opportunity to grow and mature in relationships. The next time you are confronted with an opportunity to cause embarrassment for another, realize you have a choice of words and actions.

Let's look at this another way. Would you deliberately seek to embarrass someone who can retaliate with greater embarrassment to you? Would you embarrass your employer? Would you embarrass your pastor? Would you deliberately embarrass your Lord? One of the things I've noticed about people who enjoy picking on other people is that they carefully pick their subjects. Most of the "embarrassers" rarely pick on an "embarrassee" who can retaliate in kind or with greater consequence. Which is another way of saying that the decision to embarrass another is a matter of choice. It can be controlled, it can be modified, it can be changed into something positive in a relationship.

Gerald G. Jampolsky, M.D., writes: "I am responsible for what I see, I choose the feelings I experience, and I decide upon the goal I would achieve. And everything that seems to happen to me, I ask for, and receive as I have asked."[1]

Responsibility for my actions is one sure sign of maturity. When I choose to be responsible I choose to be mature. When I choose to be mature I choose to love, which is much the same analogy the Apostle lays on us. "When I was a child, I talked like a child, I thought like a child, I reasoned like a child. When I became a man (woman), I put childish ways behind me" (1 Cor. 13:11). The choice to be the cause of embarrassment toward another comes out of a childish way of thinking and acting. It's our choice to put that away and grow up! If we are to live the most excellent way, there is not a place for this type of pettiness or meanness in any way, shape, or form. Upon a careful reading of the Gospels, I can find no situation in which Jesus Christ resorted to this type of behavior. He spoke the truth in love. He was up front and to the point. He did not embarrass others who came to Him for help or answers. Yes, He made them think, He made them see the truth, He called some of them "whited sepulchers," which may have caused some to feel uncomfortable, but there was not a trace of deliberately caused shame for anybody. In fact, He encouraged the weak, the young, the hurting, the vulnerable, and the innocent to come to Him. He didn't put them down, He lifted them up. That's one of the reasons that Jesus is so appealing to all people.

Some years ago, the late Grady Nutt told the story

about a young family who invited the new preacher and his wife over for Sunday dinner. The mother of the home was very concerned that it be a perfect affair. She drilled the children for days in advance about the proper behavior. Finally, when the day came, and the meal was cooked, everyone was invited to come into the dining room. The table was set out with a white lace tablecloth, the good china, silverware, centerpiece, candles — everything. They sat down at this formal table and the father said the blessing. When the blessing was over the little nine-year-old daughter reached for her glass of iced tea and knocked it over.

The little brother jumped to get out of the way and knocked his over, too. There was an awkward moment of silence as everybody kind of looked to the mother, realizing how disappointed she was. She had gone to so much trouble, and now there was this huge stain in the middle of the white lace tablecloth. But before anybody could say anything, the father flipped over his tea and started to laugh. The preacher caught on and flipped over his tea and started to laugh. The preacher's wife knocked over her glass of tea and started to laugh. And everybody looked to the mother, and finally with an expression of resignation, she picked up her glass and just dumped it out in the middle of the table, and everybody around the table roared with laughter.

Then the father looked down at his nine-year-old daughter right beside him and he winked at her. And as she laughed embarrassingly, she looked up at her father and winked back. But as she did it flicked a tear off of her cheek and it rolled down her face. She looked up almost worshipfully at a father who loved her enough to be sensitive enough to save her from one of life's most embarrassing moments.

REAL LOVE PROTECTS FROM EMBARRASSMENT

Real love in action will do all that is possible to save people from experiencing those embarrassing moments. Love is considerate, love is caring enough to protect as much as possible and not add to the difficulty of life. The opposite of causing embarrassment is to put others at ease, to encourage self-confidence, to lift, and to calm. At times that can be a large order, but so necessary to loving relationships. What a way to open the door to a person whom you are seeking to win to the Lord Jesus Christ and His church.

One of the major characteristics of love is that "it always protects" (1 Cor. 13:7). It will always protect the tender feelings of people we love. It will do its best to protect from those most embarrassing *faux pas* of life. "Always" indicates that it is a constant watch, a constant awareness, an on-going part of human relationships. This is one of the attractions of love. It's one of those little things that make life tolerable and livable and bearable and fun and satisfying. "I know this is maybe not thought of" as a major concern . . . but in keeping the oil of human relationships flowing, it is important!

Love that is really love will do all that is possible to avoid what may prove to be embarrassing to others. Even at great sacrifice and cost it will go the second mile, it will do the nice thing, the accommodating action, so that others may be spared.

Dr. Richard Selzer, who has written some gripping books based on his life as a doctor, relates the following life experience:

> I stand by the bed where a young woman lies, her face post-operative, her mouth twisted in palsy, clownish. A tiny

twig of the facial nerve, the one to the muscles of her mouth has been severed. She will be thus from now on. The surgeon had followed with religious fervor the curve of her flesh; I promise you that. Nevertheless, to remove the tumor in her cheek, I had cut the little nerve. Her young husband is in the room. He stands on the opposite side of the bed, and together they seem to dwell in the evening lamplight, isolated from me, private. Who are they, I ask myself, he and this wry-mouth I have made, who gaze at and touch each other so generously, greedily?

The young woman speaks. "Will my mouth always be like this?" she asks.

"Yes," I say, "it will. It is because the nerve was cut."

She nods and is silent. But the young man smiles. "I like it," he says. "It is kind of cute."

All at once I know who he is. I understand, and I lower my gaze. One is not bold in an encounter with a god. Unmindful, he bends to kiss her crooked mouth, and I am so close I can see how he twists his own lips to accommodate to hers, to show her that their kiss still works.[2]

Love . . . DOES NOT EMBARRASS OTHERS!

12

Love . . . Is Not Arrogant

Pedro was a creep, there is not a better word to describe him. The missionary who tells this story, Dale Bishop, on assignment to Colombia, confesses he would duck into a store and go out the back whenever he saw Pedro coming his way.

Pedro was one of those slick sort of characters, always after a fast buck. After several contacts with him, Bishop began to despise him.

"Lord, Pedro is a hopeless, despicable man. Take him. Send him away. I simply can't stand him." At least Bishop was honest with God.

Wrestling with the problem over a period of weeks, the missionary began to see that *he* himself must change.

He recognized he had to at least love Pedro "in the Lord."

One day he greeted Pedro on the street. They talked and Pedro invited the missionary to have a Coke with him. They talked further and Bishop began to see Pedro as a fellow human being, a man with feelings, a man for whom Christ died.

One morning the missionary awoke and found that God had changed him. He actually *loved* Pedro . . . more than simply "in the Lord." While he acknowledges that they probably will never be best friends, he had *willed* to love Pedro, and the love had come.

Loving unlovable people is never an easy assignment. But when coming in contact with those unlovable kinds of people, it's so easy to put on an air of superiority and lift ourselves above the demands of love, all the while excusing our own lousy behavior because the other person is so different. This is nothing short of arrogance.

According to the dictionary, arrogance is "a feeling of superiority or an offensive exhibition of it." Also, it's "presumptuous or overbearing conduct or statements, resulting from such a feeling."

There are a whole bunch of words and synonyms that flesh out the attitude and meaning of what it is to be arrogant: overbearing, haughty, presumptuous, pretentious, imperious, high-and-mighty, vain, conceited, egotistical, self-important, self-assuming, swaggering, insolent, disdainful, contemptuous, scornful, lordly, pompous, and supercilious. Had enough? What a list! We could add such things as loftiness, bluster, and braggadocio. When we see such things in others it repulses us. I do not like to be around arrogant people — do you? Talk about a turnoff in personal relations!

INHERENT ARROGANCE

There always seem to be people in our circle of acquaintances who, because of their attitudes or lifestyle, receive an attitude of arrogance from us. It is a human tendency. It's been inherent in the human animal from the beginning of time. In the account of Cain and Abel — the first murder — there is a generous dose of arrogance present. Cain lashed out at his brother in anger and contempt, which resulted in the cold-blooded murder of his brother.

Arrogance in any of its forms will be just as deadly to personal relationships. If it weren't so deadly it would be humorous. What have we, in and of ourselves, to be proud about? The air we breathe is on loan from God. None of us has the ability or talent to go it alone through life. There is an equality about all of us — we are all helpless.

I become a very small package when I am bordered on the north, south, east, and west by me. Not only is that a small package, it's also a selfish package of emptiness.

A new lawyer was settling into his office on the first day of his practice, and spotted a prospective client walking in the door. He decided he should look busy so he picked up the phone and started talking in a voice loud enough to be heard by the man approaching: "Look, Harry, about that amalgamation deal. I think I better run down to the factory and handle it personally. Yes . . . no . . . I don't think three million will swing it. We better have Rogers from Seattle meet us there. Okay. Call you back later." He then looked up at the visitor and said, "Good morning, how may I help you?"

The prospective client said, "You can't help me at

all. I'm here from the phone company to hook up your phone."

At this juncture I offer a quote from Paul Eldridge: "We hate the hypocrite more keenly than the mere liar because the hypocrite adds to his lie the lacquer of flattery, which we are gullible enough to accept as tribute to our merit."

I'm reminded of a cartoon with an office setting, in which the boss is shown slamming his fist on the desk and shouting, "I want to shun publicity, but I want people to know I shun publicity!"

Someone once rightly observed, "It's a shame that when success turns a person's head it does not also wring the neck just a bit."

It seems that hardly anybody can be completely free of the temptation to be proud, arrogant, and a bit disdainful. A French monk bemoaned the fact that his order was not as famous as the Jesuits for scholarship, or the Trappists for silence and good works. "But," he concluded, "when it comes to humility, we're tops."

THE FIRST STEP

Okay, so we have this very large obstacle to loving relationships in human interactions. What do we do about it? Is there any cure for arrogant people? I believe there is and it's quite simple. (I didn't say easy, I said simple.) It begins with a first step, one that needs to be taken if any of the human ills are to be changed: acknowledgment.

Until and unless there is an honest acknowledging on the part of the arrogant person, there's not much hope for correction. The songwriter captured this in a line, "It's me, it's me, Oh Lord, standing in the need of prayer . . . not my brother or my sister, but it's me, Oh Lord!"

Repeat after me: "I am arrogant, full of pride, and show disdain for others instead of showing love to them!" That hurts, but that is honest. It's the pivotal point in doing an about-face. When this is done with humility, there is great hope for the future!

> *Someone once rightly observed, "It's a shame that when success turns a person's head it does not also wring the neck just a bit."*

Just as people who are working with alcoholics tell us there is no cure or hope until this step has been taken, there is not much hope in replacing arrogance with love in our own living without confession.

Sometimes we try a shortcut in our 'fessing up: "Okay, there is a bit of arrogance in my living . . . but it's not nearly as bad as so-and-so. Now, there's somebody who needs the cure!" Just how much arrogance does it take to be arrogant? Can a woman be a little bit pregnant? In God's sight, sin is sin. It's not a question of how much . . . sin is sin. Arrogance is arrogance! How much does it take to spoil life for others?

A wise man said, "If you put a spoonful of wine in a barrel full of sewage, you have sewage. But if you put a spoonful of sewage in a barrel full of wine, you have . . . sewage."

The root cause of bragging is found in the Scriptures. "For everything in the world — the cravings of sinful man, the lust of his eyes and the boasting of what he has and does — comes not from the Father but from the world" (1 John 2:16). Did you pick it up? "The boasting of what he/she has and does...." What we *have* and what we *do* are sources of boasting. In reality we have so little and have done so little. What do we have and do that is worth being arrogant about?

I'm pretty sure that none of us has touched and molded the world nearly as much as the ancient king, Nebuchadnezzar. He built and ruled over what may well have been the greatest world power ever on earth. Let's listen in on his expression of arrogance: "Twelve months later, as the king was walking on the roof of the royal palace of Babylon, he said, 'Is not this the great Babylon I have built as the royal resident, by my mighty power and for the glory of my majesty?' " (Dan. 4:29-30).

Very likely he was making this little speech from the rooftop of the "Hanging Gardens," which was considered one of the seven wonders of the ancient world. Nebuchadnezzar had revived the city's fortunes in what can be considered a great human accomplishment.

How did God take to his little speech? Read on: "The words were still on his lips when a voice came from heaven, 'This is what is decreed for you, King Nebuchadnezzar: Your royal authority has been taken from you. You will be driven away from people . . .' " (Dan. 4:31-32).

We can deduce from this that God does not take lightly to boasting, braggadocio, and pride. There was instant judgment! Thank God that He is also kind, loving, and long-suffering to us. There's still time to make the correction in your living. From this we can also see that if we don't humble ourselves, God can do the job quite easily.

In the life of this king, did the cure take? After a seven year period we pick up the story: "At the end of that time, I, Nebuchadnezzar, raised my eyes toward heaven, and my sanity was restored. Then I praised the Most High. Now I, Nebuchadnezzar, praise and exalt and glorify the King of heaven, because everything He does is right and all His ways are just [note this statement carefully] *and those who walk in pride He is able to humble*" (Dan. 4:34,37).

Talk about a sobering life lesson to all the prideful, boastful people who walk and live on this earth. The choice is quite simple: Either I acknowledge the pride of my life or God can. He may not do it quickly in the here and now, but it will be done. I remind you, a day and time is coming when, "at the name of Jesus every knee should bow, in heaven and on earth and under the earth, and every tongue confess that Jesus Christ is Lord, to the glory of God the Father" (Phil. 2:10-11). This entire section on the epitome of humility is from Philippines. Paul begins with: "Your attitude should be the same as that of Jesus Christ" (Phil. 2:5). There is hope for all of us!

One of the major benefits of willingly confessing my sin of arrogance is a true perspective on life. Who and what is important? We already know for sure that it's not what I have or what I do or what I say.

A missionary who was involved in translation work was speaking to an American crowd about some of the difficulties in translating the word "pride," or at least the concept, in the particular tribe he had been assigned to. After much thought and some prayer, he came up with the idea to use their word for "the ears are too far apart." So he was conveying the idea of an "inflated head," which is pretty hard to improve on.

A wealthy man invited a number of guests for a feast. These were the "important" people, politically, of his area. They wanted to be seen in his presence and cultivate his favor. It was obvious his was the ornate chair at the head of the table. There were no place cards. On purpose, he excused himself for a moment or two and the butler announced they would soon be served and all should find their places at the table. The confusion that took place as each guest seated himself according to his own pride in his position was humorous to watch. They all wanted the place of importance in relation to the host. When they had all been seated, this philanthropist entered the room, picked up his own chair, and moved it to the opposite end of the table! Seems to me that the Bible says something about seating ourselves at the places of honor as a life action we should not indulge in.

Out of World War II comes this telling story about Charles H. Kasserman:

> As we were leaving Pearl Harbor on a patrol craft, we found ourselves on a collision course with an enormous aircraft carrier. After an emergency backdown, and a sigh of relief, we were left standing on the bow watching the mammoth carrier pass by, less than 50 feet away. A patrol craft is only 100 feet long, and our crew stood on the deck feeling very insignificant. However, our pride was saved by our ship's mate. He took a megaphone in hand and yelled, "Our skipper can lick your skipper!"

Oh, we humans! We just have to salvage something, "save face" somehow, keep our pride intact! And in the process show our humanness and stupidity and vulnerability.

THE NEXT STEP

So, I humbly have suggested that the cure for arrogance begins with acknowledgment, which needs to be followed by perspective, and to make it significant and meaningful, cement your decision with repentance and action.

Supposedly this is a true incident, but I cannot find the source, so here goes the story anyway: A young lady visited the preserved home of Beethoven. She boldly slipped under the rope surrounding the piano, seated herself on the bench and began playing Beethoven's piano. Then she spoke to the shocked museum attendant in front of the small crowd of people, "I suppose every musician who comes here wants to play this piano."

He then explained to her that recently the great Paderewski was visiting there and some with him in his group, recognizing him, had insisted that he play that piano. He replied, "No, I do not feel worthy to play the great master's piano."

Actions determine whether or not we have an attitude of humility. Actions can make liars out of our words. True repentance will be exhibited in loving words and actions. To be living and acting in humility takes a greater power than our own self-will. Ours is a world which praises self: self-importance, self-awareness, and the self-made person. To get ahead we are challenged to place ourselves ahead of others, put others down, and act from the power base of superiority. It doesn't work and hasn't worked.

Let me conclude this chapter with two stories — one showing the destructiveness of acting from a stance of arrogance, and the other of acting out of humility.

Elmer Kelen turned to leave the studio of a

young Hungarian artist, Arpad Sebesy. He was angry, arrogant, disdainful, and contemptuous as he shot out his parting words. "That's a rotten portrait and I refuse to pay for it!" The artist was crushed. He had spent weeks on this painting and now the 500 pengos he was going to lose on the deal flashed through his mind. Bitterly he recalled the millionaire had only posed three times, so that the painting had to be done virtually from memory. Still, he didn't think it was such a bad likeness.

Before the proud millionaire left his studio the artist called out, "One minute. Will you give me a letter saying you refused the portrait because it doesn't resemble you?" Glad to get off the hook so easily, Kelen agreed and wrote the letter.

Some months later the Society of Hungarian Artists opened its exhibition at the Gallery of Fine Arts in Budapest. Soon afterwards Kelen's phone began to ring. Within half an hour he appeared at the gallery and headed for the wing where a Sebesy painting was on display. It was the one he had rejected.

He glanced at the title and his face turned purple with rage. Storming into the office of the gallery manager, he demanded the portrait be removed at once. The manager explained quietly that all of the paintings were under contract to remain in the gallery the full six weeks of the exhibit.

Kelen raged, "But it will make me the laughing stock of Budapest. It's libelous. I'll sue!"

The manager turned to his desk, drew out the letter Kelen had written at Sebesy's request, and said coolly, "Just a moment. Since you yourself admit the painting does not resemble you, you have no jurisdiction over its fate."

In desperation, Kelen offered to buy the painting, only to find the price now ten times that of the original figure. With his reputation at stake, Kelen immediately wrote out a check for 5,000 pengos!

Not only did the artist sell the rejected portrait to the man who had originally commissioned it, and get far more than the original price, he had achieved his revenge simply by exhibiting it with this title: "Portrait of a Thief!"

Contrast that story with this one as told by Donald Grey Barnhouse:

When Chief Justice Charles Evans Hughes moved to Washington, DC, to take up his duties as chief justice, he transferred his membership letter to a Baptist church in the area. His father had been a Baptist minister, and he also made a profession of faith in Christ. It was the custom for all new members to come to the front of the sanctuary at the close of the worship service.

The first to be called that morning was Ah Sing, a Chinese laundryman who had moved to the capital from the West Coast. He took his place at the far side of the church. As the dozen or so other people were called forward they stood at the opposite side of the church, leaving Ah Sing standing alone. But when Chief Justice Hughes was called, he took his place beside the laundryman.

When the minister had welcomed the group into the church fellowship he turned to the congregation and said, "I do not want this congregation to miss this remarkable illustration of the fact that at the cross of Jesus Christ the ground is level."

Barnhouse commented: "Mr. Hughes behaved like a true Christian. He took his place beside the laundryman, and by his act he prevented embarrassment to the humble Chinese; he showed, too, the love of Christ . . . he had this gift of standing by."

Love . . . IS NOT ARROGANT!

13

Love . . . Is Not Selfish

I
ME
MINE
MYSELF
ME-FIRST
MINE-FIRST-LAST
MYSELF-FIRST-LAST-AND-ALWAYS

Have you walked into a bookstore lately? Just saunter over to the "self-help" section. Books on improving ourselves have become best sellers. We give them as gifts, we believe them as gospel. Books on how to get to the top, how to not let anyone walk on you, how to use the organization to satisfy your selfish needs — there seems to be a new book each day. We want to know how to look out for number one, always, and in every circumstance. Admit it, come clean — we are submerged in the philosophy of gross, obscene selfishness.

Ours is the "me first" generation.

> *We want enough of God to give us warm fuzzies, but not enough of God to transform our actions.*

In all of this clamor is it possible to still be sensitive to others, to be aware of the call of God in our lives? Sadly, selfishness has always been a deterrent to loving relationships. We really get uncomfortable with the still small voice of God, the unspoken demands to live for others, and the urgent needs in others who haven't been as loud as the cries of putting self first.

Wilbur Rees captures that essence with his snippet of sarcasm: "I would like to buy $3 worth of God, please, not enough to explode my soul or disturb my sleep, but just enough to equal a cup of warm milk or a snooze in the sunshine. I don't want enough of Him to make me love a black man or pick beets with a migrant. I want ecstasy, not transformation; I want the warmth of the womb, not a new birth. I want a pound of the Eternal in a paper sack. I would like to buy $3 worth of God, please."[1]

We want enough of God to give us warm fuzzies, but not enough of God to transform our actions. Put it in a sack . . . just enough to allow me to sleep at night, but not enough to change a lifestyle. And just because we claim to be Christians is no guarantee that this battle with selfishness has been won. It is one of those inherent, ingrained, deeply rooted problems with character. Selfishness. Slice the soul of any one of us and in too many you'll find a deadly seed of self, a grasping nature, a put-me-first motivator.

Would you allow me a disclaimer, just a break to bring a bit of perspective into our equation? Self-esteem and selfishness are not the same. A balanced self-esteem will give strength to living which we all need. If you don't believe yourself, who will? And don't compare a poor self-image to living in humility. We all need to have a confidence that God is in us, walking with us, caring for us, and loving us, so we can become productive people in His world. No, don't mix up the strong, balanced self-esteem with selfishness that manifests itself in pride.

One more thought in this same vein: Christianity will not guarantee all pride is gone. Lots of Christians are fighting this battle. There's a subtleness about pride that makes it hard to recognize. Evangelicals have an air about them — about us (let's make it personal) — that somehow we have the right answers about life and theology. We don't say it, but it's such a comforting thing to be able to look down our spiritual noses at those poor people who do not see the light as we have found it! Come on, let's face it for what it is.

The late Bishop Fulton J. Sheen was asked to describe his "most inspiring moment." Here's what he wrote:

> A few years ago I visited a leper colony in Africa. I brought with me 500 small silver crucifixes to give to each victim of the dread disease. The first leper who came up to me

had only a stump of his left arm. The right arm and hand were full of those telltale white open sores of leprosy. I held the crucifix a few inches above that hand and let it drop into the palm. At that moment there were 501 lepers in that camp, and the most leprous of them all was *myself.* I had taken the symbol of redemption, of Divine Love for man, of the humiliation of Divinity, and had refused to identify myself with all that that symbol implied. It is so easy to love humanity in *general* but so difficult sometimes to love a *particular* man. It is easy to help the lepers, but when one meets a *particular* leper, then a special effort is required.

Seeing myself in the full shame of refusing to identify myself with this victim, I looked at the crucifix in the putrid mass of his hand and realized that I, too, must become one with suffering humanity. Then I pressed my hand to his hand with the symbol of love between us, and continued to do it for the other 499 lepers.[2]

THE BIRTHPLACE OF PRIDE

Before we can really deal with any problem, especially one as strong as pride, it helps if we have background on and understanding about what we are dealing with. To do that with self takes us on a journey across time and place to the ancient, frightening, most beautiful setting imaginable: the Garden of Eden. It's almost impossible to imagine a place totally free of sin and pride, with the most favorable circumstances under which to establish and maintain a loving relationship.

An absolutely unselfish setting. The verification is in the narrative, "The man and his wife were both naked, and they felt no shame" (Gen. 2:25).

Theirs was an openness — physically, emotionally, and mentally — and they had a total lack of self-consciousness with each other. Think about it: no sin, therefore no "self"-ishness. None! Until . . . and you already know the rest of the story . . . sin entered the picture. "Then the eyes of both of them were opened, and they realized they were naked" (3:7). Notice their *eyes* were opened. For the first time they became *"self"*-conscious. This is where it all began: self-concern, self-awareness, self-love, self-seeking, self-conceit, and self-importance. If this is the origin, how was it acted out in behavior? This man and woman, for the first time, began looking out for number one: "Then the man and his wife heard the sound of the LORD God as He was walking in the garden in the cool of the day, and they hid from the LORD God among the trees of the garden" (3:8).

Did Eve look out for Adam? Did Adam help Eve? Each got busy for themselves. Each attempted to hide from God. Each did their own thing. They played one of the favorite games of all time — Hide and Seek. But with God? That's a no-win kind of situation! How can you hide from God?

It continues with terminology we easily recognize as self-oriented: "But the LORD God called to the man, 'Where are you?' He answered, 'I heard you in the garden, and I was afraid because I was naked; so I hid' " (3:9-10). Notice — no mention of Eve, the "bone of my bones and flesh of my flesh" as discussed in Genesis 2:23. It's now each man for himself.

That's not all. Adam mixes half-truths with truth.

He doesn't come clean with God, but points the blame to another. He concealed his own act of willful disobedience. Adam, from that point in history, will no more be able to function without self awareness in relationship to God and to others around him.

God moved in a bit closer, and when cornered these two hurled accusations at each other, the serpent, and against God. The man said, "The woman you put here with me..." (Gen. 3:12). Nice shot, Adam. You got both your mate and God with the same volley! The woman said, "The serpent deceived me..." (3:13). Well, anyway, the pattern hasn't changed much over the years, has it?

Oh, we may have refined this first exchange a bit, but look at any segment of human history to see the ongoing manifestation of "self." We cover up, accuse, excuse, deny, hide, lie, dominate, criticize, and slice and dice people! So, what's new?

"Me? I'm not arrogant, I just have strong opinions!"

"Me? I'm not judging, I'm just a fruit inspector!"

"Me? I'm not angry, I just have convictions!"

"Me? I'm not critical, I'm just expressing myself on the subject!"

If you think Christians are not self-serving, watch our actions in getting out of a crowded parking lot on Sunday morning. Check out the lines at the cashier. Observe the maneuvering at your next church annual business meeting. See, we've perfected our little game because we've had so much practice. You learn quickly how to look out for *self* in the nursery. "Mine ... mine ... mine" is the cry of little tots! School isn't much better as you continue learning how to look out for *self*, if you don't get any other life lessons. It continues on through college, then through marriage, and on through the life vocation. Some of us have developed real finesse and have refined the art to new highs. We didn't catch it by chance, like the mumps or measles. It's congenital. It's the nature from Adam we were born with, which is not an excuse to continue living for self.

THE CURE FOR PRIDE

Jesus Christ — the virgin-born Son of God, sinless, pure, Deity — lived among us, and showed us how to live above self, how to conquer self, and gave us direction on how to deal with self. Jesus laid out a new direction: "When the ten heard about this, they were indignant with the two brothers. Jesus called them together and said, 'You know that the rulers of the Gentiles lord it over them, and their high officials exercise authority over them. *NOT SO WITH YOU* (my emphasis). Instead, whoever wants to be first must be your slave — just as the Son of Man did not come to be served, but to serve, and to give his life as a ransom for many" (Matt. 20:24-28).

Me be a servant? You've got to be kidding! We are not interested in anything that's not geared to elevating self. Jesus said the way to cure selfishness is by taking an opposite role. Instead of being on top, He said go to the end of the line. Don't ask people to serve you, you serve them. It's simple in concept, yet difficult in reality.

Leonard Bernstein, famous orchestra conductor, as part of a performance on television, was interviewed during an informal part of the program. One of the questioners asked, "Mr. Bernstein, what is the most difficult instrument to play?"

He responded with humor, "Second fiddle. I can get plenty of first violinists, but to find one who plays second violin with as much enthusiasm, or second French horn, or second flute, now that's a problem. And yet if no one plays second, we have no harmony."

Jesus is our supreme model when it comes to living out the selfless life. The apostle Paul wrote: "Do nothing out of selfish ambition or vain conceit, but in humility consider others better than yourselves. Each of you should look not only to your own interests, but also to the interests of others. Your attitude should be the same as that of Christ Jesus" (Phil. 2:3-5)

Contrast that with the philosophy of today! In the simplest terms Jesus told us to serve, think of others, give to others, and love others.

The Rev. Charlie Webster shares this story about his days at Princeton Seminary:

> A professor of ethics asked for volunteers for an extra assignment. At two o'clock, fifteen students gathered at Speer Library. There he divided the group of fifteen into three groups of five. They were given envelopes. The first group of five were given written intructions telling them to proceed immediately across campus to Stewart Hall, that they had fifteen minutes to get there and if they didn't arrive on time it would affect their grade. This was called the "High Hurry" group.
>
> A minute or two later he handed out envelopes to five others. Their instructions were to go over to Stewart Hall, but they were given 45 minutes. This was the "Medium Hurry" group.
>
> After they departed he turned over the

envelopes with instructions to the third group, the "Low Hurry" group. They were given three hours to arrive at Stewart Hall.

Not known to any of these students, the teacher had arranged with three drama students to meet them along the way, acting as people in great need. In front of Alexander Hall one of the drama students was going around covering his head with his hands and moaning out loud in great pain. As they passed by Miller Chapel they found one fellow who was on the steps laying face down as if unconscious. And finally on the very steps of Stewart Hall the third drama student was acting out an epileptic seizure.

It's interesting that of the first group *no one* stopped; of the second, two of the five stopped; and of the third fivesome, all five stopped.

Charlie's point was that maybe one of the reasons that the Good Samaritan was able to stop and help was because he had a more leisurely agenda, while the religious "pros" of Jesus' day were living in the fast lane and simply had no time for interruptions. Their calendars may well have been filled with commitments that left them no leeway.[3]

This is another way of expressing self living and selfishness. How we need to assault that sin in our lives. It means being different. It means walking to a different beat. Selfless living stands out in a crowd because so few people practice it.

> *Selfless living stands out in a crowd because so few people practice it.*

Can I remind you, once more, of our working definition of love in this book? "Love is an action directed to another person that is motivated by our relationship to Jesus Christ *and is given freely without a personal reward in mind.*"

Children in Sunday school are told that in order to experience joy, it should be spelled as "J-esus, O-thers, and Y-ou!" To slay self we need to learn what it is to be a forgiver, a forgetter, a servant, a giver, and someone who cares.

In the final word, love is nothing until it becomes an unselfish action or lifestyle. Consider this:

Just about everyone knows the Jim Brady story — how the big, bluff, quick-witted "Bear," only two months after becoming White House press secretary, was shot in the head during the attempted assassination of President Reagan, and how he has fought his way back from brain surgery and the crippling, enduring damage from the stray bullet.

Not many people know, however, about the ceaseless, selfless, single-minded, devoted love of Bob Dahlgren — a man who loved Brady like himself.

Bob Dahlgren died in his sleep, at 52 years of age. It didn't even make the morning news. But during the long months following the shooting it was Dahlgren who took the vigil with Brady's wife Sarah, through the long series of brain operations. It was Dahlgren and his wife Suzie who took the Bradys' young son into their home through the early days of the ordeal.

It was Dahlgren who helped ease the way toward recovery by arranging convivial "happy hours" with Brady's friends by his hospital bedside.

As Brady recovered and was able, in a wheelchair, to return to a semi-normal life, it was Dahlgren, always Dahlgren, who scouted out the advance arrangements, who helped load and unload his friend from the specially equipped van in which Brady did most of his traveling.

It was Dahlgren who helped Sarah field the interminable questions about Brady's health and who spent endless hours keeping Brady's friends posted on his condition, who dealt with the doctors, lawyers, exploiters, and bandwagon-climbers.

It was Dahlgren who helped organize a foundation to assure financial support for the family.

For more than four and a half years after Brady was shot, Bob Dahlgren devoted virtually all his time to the man he loved. And he did so with little recognition, and no hint of seeing anything in return. Never, ever, did Dahlgren complain. Never did he hesitate when needed. Never did he stop looking for the needs or the response of love.

As Dr. Arthur Kobrine, the surgeon who lived through Brady's long ordeal with him, once said, "Everyone should have a friend like Bob Dahlgren."

Authentic, selfless love, to be genuine, will show itself in selfless actions. It's not the thought that counts . . . it's the selfless action which counts. It's the triumph of love in action over self and selfish action.

Love . . . IS NOT SELFISH!

14

Love . . . Doesn't Remember Wrongs Suffered

On a cold winter evening a man suffered a heart attack, and after being admitted to the hospital, asked the nurse to call his daughter. He explained, "You see, I live alone and she is the only family I have."

The nurse went to phone the daughter. The daughter was quite upset and shouted over the phone, "You must not let him die! You see, Dad and I had a terrible argument almost a year ago. I haven't seen him since. All these months I've wanted to go to him for forgiveness. The last thing I said to him was 'I hate you.' " The daughter cried and then said, "I'm coming now — I'll be there in thirty minutes."

The patient went into cardiac arrest and "code blue" was sounded. The nurse prayed, "Oh, God, his daughter is coming. Don't let it end this way." The efforts of the medical team to revive the patient were fruitless. The nurse observed one of the doctors talking to the daughter outside the room. She could see the pathetic hurt in her face. The nurse took the daughter aside and said, "I'm sorry."

The daughter responded, "I never hated him, you know. I loved him, and now I want to go see him."

The nurse thought, *Why put yourself through more pain?* But she took her to the room where her father lay. The daughter went to the bed and buried her face in the sheets as she said goodbye to her deceased father. The nurse, as she tried not to look at this sad goodbye, noticed a scrap of paper on the bedside table. She picked it up and read: "My dearest Janie, I forgive you. I pray you will also forgive me. I know that you love me. I love you, too. Daddy."[1]

Oh, the hurt that arises out of holding onto wrongs suffered. Bearing a grudge may be the heaviest burden known to man.

Have you ever said, or heard another say, "I may forgive you, but I'll *never* forget?" Forgiveness without letting go of the wrong — is it really forgiveness?

So you've been wronged, somebody did you dirty, it was unjust, unwarranted, inexcusable, and reprehensible. It's probably no consolation, but most everyone else has experienced the same in their lives. The crux of the matter is what you do with the wrong. Wrongs will happen. You will be mistreated, maltreated, ill-treated, and cheated in life. We all have enemies, but the greatest enemy we face is Satan himself. He will make it his express duty to see that you are mistreated in some manner by people whom you love or should be loving. He will see to it that there is something that really hurts which you would like to hold on to, actions you are on the receiving end of that can be turned into grudges, things you choose not to forget because just the thought of revenge is so sweet.

Refusing to forget is the cornerstone of monuments to the spirit of revenge! Think with me a moment . . . how many churches are you aware of which came into existence because of a split over some issue? In the area of the upper Midwest where I was born, a church split in two over the issue of whether they should have buttons or snaps on their clothing!

Is it ever possible to really, truly forget? How can such actions be released from our memory banks?

Dr. Earl Radmacher writes:

> The human mind is a fabulous computer. As a matter of fact, no one has been able to design a computer as intricate and efficient as the human mind. Consider this: your brain is capable of recording 800 memories per second for seventy-five years without ever getting tired . . . .
>
> The point is, the brain is capable of an incredible amount of work and it retains everything it takes in. You never really forget anything; you just don't recall it. Everything is on permanent file in your brain.[2]

History is one long litany of people who refused to forget wrongs. Consider the young Jewish boy born and raised in Germany who had a profound admiration for his father. The life of this family centered around their religion. Dad was zealous in attending worship and the same was expected from the children.

While this boy was in his teens the family moved to another town in Germany. In this new town there were no synagogues and the the community leaders all attended the Lutheran church. The father announced to the family, and in particular to this son, that they would now join the Lutheran church and give up their Jewish traditions. The teen was confused, hurt, and bewildered. His disappointment soon gave way to anger, which turned to bitterness, which followed him and marked him for the rest of his life.

> *To be able to forget is more than a natural reaction, it is a supernatural action.*

When old enough he left Germany and went to England to study. He spent lots of time in the British Museum formulating his ideas and culminating in a book. In this book he fashioned a philosophy which was destined to forever change the face of the modern world. He originated the idea that religion was the "opiate of the masses." His premise was that everything could be explained in economic terms. Millions of people have lived and died and many still live under the system devised by this bitter man who refused to let go of his hurt. You've guessed his name — Karl Marx. Would it be stretching our point to say communisitic oppression came about because one man refused to let go of his wrong? I think not.

To be able to forget is more than a natural reaction, it is a *supernatural* action. I am talking about "forgetting" in the same sense that Paul the Apostle wrote: love "keeps no record of wrongs. Love does not delight in evil" (1 Cor. 13:5-6). In fact, J.B. Phillips, in his translation, carries it a bit further: "It does not keep account of evil or gloat over the wickedness of other people." If we are to be genuine people who love, we will no longer keep score.

What does it really mean to "forget," to not "remember wrongs suffered?" *Webster's Dictionary* defines "forgetting" as "disregarding intentionally: overlooking, to cease remembering or noticing." What a virtue! The ability to overlook or intentionally disregard the wrongs suffered.

Let's bring this into a tighter focus by taking a closer look at forgetting. Again, we return to Paul's writings to look at the definitive section on our subject. "If anyone else thinks he has reasons to put confidence in the flesh, I have more: circumcised . . . a Hebrew of Hebrews . . . a Pharisee . . . zeal . . . as for legalistic righteousness, faultless" (Phil. 3:4-6). Impressive materials from which to give a testimony! But his next lines bring that back into perspective. "But whatever was to my profit I now consider loss for the sake of Christ. What is more, I consider everything a loss compared to the surpassing greatness of knowing Christ Jesus my Lord, for whose sake I have lost all things" (Phil. 3:7-8). Next to Jesus Christ, everything of this life pales.

Now we move on to the focus of our subject: "Not that I have already obtained all this, or have already been made perfect, but I press on to take hold of that for which Christ Jesus took hold of me . . . but one thing I do: Forgetting what is behind and straining toward what is ahead, I press on toward the goal to win the prize for which God has called me heavenward in Christ Jesus" (Phil. 3:12-14). Out of these verses there are at least three concepts which can give us a handle on letting go of the past, *forgetting* what is past and turning it around to move with a positive stride into the future.

VULNERABILITY

How refreshing it is to see someone willing to become vulnerable. Hear Paul as he says, "not that I have already obtained all this or have already been made perfect . . . I do not consider myself yet to have taken hold of it." Not only is this refreshing, it is rare. How difficult it is to admit to limitations, to admit we don't have all the answers, to admit we are not the authority on every subject, to admit to failures, or to admit personal hurts.

Not only is this rare, but it makes us much easier to live with. To become vulnerable is the attitude of the person who is serious about the actions of love. Not everything will turn out wonderful, not all of what we experience in life will end the way we want it to end. We are human and being human we sin and fall and fail. What about your strengths? Would you be willing to hide them? What about your weaknesses? Are you willing for others to see these? When I become vulnerable and human, barriers come down. The paradox of this gospel of Jesus Christ is that when we are weak we become strong. When we are vulnerable we are approachable, softer, kinder, more accessible to others. Being vulnerable is the first step to take towards not remembering the wrongs.

MEEKNESS

Are you one of those people who live in the past? Not Paul. "Forgetting what is behind" and not dwelling on what has been a past accomplishment or an offense, he is free to move into the future and present. Here is meekness in action.

Have you ever taken the time to look at some of Paul's past? Consider these words from 2 Corinthians 11:23-27: "I have worked much harder, been in prison more frequently, been flogged more severely, and been exposed to death again and again. Five times I received from the Jews the forty lashes minus one. Three times I was beaten with rods, once I was stoned, three times I was shipwrecked. I have been constantly on the move. I have been in danger from rivers, bandits, my own countrymen, Gentiles, in the city, in the country, at sea, and from false brothers. I have labored and toiled and have often gone without sleep; I have known hunger and thirst and have often gone without food; I have been cold and naked."

How many people could have been on Paul's "hate list?" Who were the people who did him the wrongs of beatings, floggings, death threats, imprisonment, and starvation? If anybody ever had good reason to remember the wrongs of injustice, it must have been Paul.

Yet as we read about his life we find no hate list, but a list of people to whom he expressed loving actions. Take the time to read some of his closing instructions in his epistles. If Paul had spent his time nursing the wounds of his past and taking revenge on his enemies, would he have been the man we remember today? Think of what would have been lost to the kingdom of Heaven if Paul had spent his time and energy on getting even!

Paul, in his meekness, purposefully forgot all the wrongs, injustices, inequities, hurts, and betrayals of his past.

There's another man from the Bible who illustrates this principle — Joseph. You remember his story of betrayal, rejection, being sold into slavery and put in prison, and being considered dead by his father. Yet Joseph survived, even thrived through all this adversity.

Joseph and his wife, Asenath, named their first born "Manasseh." Explaining the name, Joseph said, "It is because God has made me forget all my trouble and all my father's household" (Gen. 41:51). It's only with God's help that we can really let go of those wrongs!

Hear this same concept from the prophet: "Do not be afraid; you will not suffer shame. Do not fear disgrace; you will not be humiliated. You will forget the shame of your youth and remember no more the reproach of your widowhood" (Isa. 54:4).

Do you have a troubled youth? God himself will take the place of those hurtful memories. Here's the promise: "For your maker is your husband — the Lord Almighty is his name — the Holy One of Israel is your Redeemer; he is called the God of all the earth" (54:5). Have you lost a loved one? God has promised to take the place of the one lost no matter how it may have happened or hurt. There's help to enable us to forget. Meekness is the key that turns the lock so that God can enter your life to help you put behind you the pains of the past. It is possible to forget, with God's help!

Now we must add one more ingredient to vulnerability and meekness to allow us to not hold on to the wrongs out of our past.

TENACITY

Tenacity, perseverance, determination, and spunk simply drip from Paul's statement, "Straining toward what is ahead, I press on toward the goal" (Phil. 3:14). Our challenge is to not get bogged down in the baggage of the past so we are free to move on in life. Dealing constantly with the wrongs of the past will prevent any kind of positive movement into a future. People who are wrapped in yesterday's injustices are petty, small, and unproductive. Forget it! Leave it behind!

How did this work out in Paul's life and ministry? Would you accept one of his own evaluations? He said, "The time has come for my departure. I have fought the good fight, I have finished the race, I have kept the faith. Now there is in store for me the crown of righteousness, which the Lord, the righteous judge, will award to me on that day — and not only to me, but also to all who have longed for his appearing" (2 Tim. 4:6-8).

You may be thinking, "That was Paul, but you don't know me or my situation." And to be honest, I don't know about you or your situation... but God does. The principles are the same for all of us. Human nature is tenacious at this point in that we don't want to let go of those wrongs because those may be all we have of our past. We would rather hang on than to move on. With God's help and a decision on your part, you too can let go of the past to move into a new tomorrow. God has grace for all your hurts and wrongs and injustices in your past.

Going through the steps to forgetting is pretty much a solo flight. If you give to someone, there's at least another person with whom you are sharing a mutual experience, but when you forget it's an individual action.

Now, just a moment for a question: *Is there some-thing or someone from your past you are refusing to forgive or forget?* How about taking this time to deal with that situation. Be honest with God. Ask Him to help with the pain and emotion.

One more question: *Am I drowning myself in self pity so that my present is paralyzed with bitterness?* If so, why would you want to live the rest of your life with such a burden? It's never too late to change. It's never too late to begin doing what you should have been doing all along.

The essence of what I have been saying has been captured in a true story as told by John Edmund Haggai. It's the story of tragedy and triumph; of dealing with horrible injustices. Mr. Haggai tells it best in his own words:

The Lord graciously blessed us with a precious son. He was paralyzed and able to sit in his wheelchair only with the assistance of full-length body braces. One of the nation's most respected gynecologists and obstetricians brought him into the world. Tragically this man — overcome by grief — sought to find the answer in a bourbon bottle rather than in a blessed Bible. Due to the doctor's intoxication at the time of delivery, he inexcusably bungled his responsibility. Several of the baby's bones were broken. His leg was pulled out at the growing center. Needless abuse, resulting in hemorrhaging of the brain, was inflicted upon the little fellow. (Let me pause long enough to say that this is no indictment upon doctors. I thank God for doctors. This man was a tragic exception. He was banned from practice in some hospitals, and . . . he committed suicide.)

During the first year of the little lad's life, eight doctors said he could not possibly survive. For the first two years of his life my wife had to feed him every three hours with a Brecht feeder. It took a half-hour to prepare for the feeding and it took another half-hour to clean up and put him back to bed. Not once during that time did she ever get out of the house for any diversion whatsoever. Never did she get more than two hours sleep at one time.

My wife, formerly Christine Barker of Bristol, Virginia, had once been acclaimed by some of the nation's leading musicians as one of the outstanding contemporary female vocalists in America. From the time she was thirteen she had been popular as a singer and was constantly in the public eye. She rejected some fancy offers with even fancier incomes to marry an aspiring Baptist pastor with no church to pastor!

Then, after five years of marriage, tragedy struck! The whole episode was so unnecessary. From a life of public service she was now marooned within the walls of our home. Her beautiful voice no longer enraptured public audiences with the story of Jesus, but was now silenced, or at best, muted to the subdued humming of lullabies.

Had it not been for her spiritual maturity, whereby she laid hold of the resources of God and lived one day at a time, this heart-rending experience would long since have caused an emotional breakdown.

John Edmund, Jr., our little son, lived more than twenty years. We rejoice that he committed his heart and life to Jesus Christ and gave evidence of a genuine concern for the things of the Lord. I attribute his commitment to Jesus Christ and his wonderful disposition to the sparkling radiance of an emotionally mature, Christ-centered mother who has mastered the discipline of living one day at a time. Never have I — nor has anyone else — heard a word of complaint from her. The people who know her concur that at thirty-five years of age, and after having been subjected to more grief than many people twice her age, she possessed sparkle that would be the envy of any high school senior, and the radiance and charm for which any debutante would gladly give a fortune.

Seize today. Live for today. Wring it dry of every opportunity.[3]

Love . . . DOESN'T REMEMBER WRONGS SUF-FERED!

15

Love . . . Does Not Get Angry Easily

The great maestro Toscanini was as well-known for his ferocious temper as for his outstanding musicianship. When members of his orchestra played badly he would pick up anything in sight and hurl it to the floor and stomp on it. During one rehearsal a flat note caused the genius to grab his valuable watch and smash it beyond repair.

Shortly afterward he received from his devoted musicians a luxurious velvet-lined box containing two watches. One was a beautiful gold timepiece, the other was a cheap one on which was inscribed, "For rehearsals only!"[1]

164 • *Love 101*

Studies at Columbia University revealed that under ordinary circumstances the average man loses his temper about six times a week, while a woman, under the same conditions, will lose her cool only three times a week. The research also showed that men are more likely to become angry over inanimate objects, whereas women generally hit the ceiling over actions of other people.

Dr. Walter Cannon, a pioneer in psychosomatic medicine at Harvard University, describes the physical symptoms of anger like this: "Respiration deepens; the heart beats more rapidly; the arterial pressure rises; the blood is shifted from the stomach and intestines to the heart, central nervous system, and the muscles; the processes of the alimentary canal cease; sugar is freed from the reserves in the liver; the spleen contracts and discharges its contents of concentrated corpuscles, and adrenaline is secreted." The body will stay in this condition for hours or even days, depending on the provocation. Anger is triggered by the mind, but the body bears the brunt of the pain. Prolonged or persistant anger can result in high blood pressure, ulcers, and a whole host of other symptoms and sicknesses.

The biblical text from which we have been working says that love "is not easily angered" (1 Cor. 13:5). Why not? Love has found a better way.

What is the root cause of anger? Anger happens when one or more of our personal "rights" have been violated. It's a normal reaction. Each of us has a list of personal rights, real or imagined, which when violated causes us to react in anger. If we are going to be effective in dealing with anger, we must deal with our rights. We can conquer our anger if we can find a way to handle our rights.

We are to submit our rights to God, allowing Him

to direct our path of life. This trail — the submission of personal rights — has already been blazed. We see our example in the letter of Paul to the Philippians: "Your attitude should be the same as that of Christ Jesus." (Phil. 2: 5). Let's take a closer look to see how this works out in daily life.

CHRIST WILLINGLY YIELDED HIS RIGHT TO WEALTH

There is no way we can begin to comprehend the splendor or wealth of heaven. The tremendous wealth Jesus was willing to leave behind can only be hinted at in the Word of God.

Here is an exciting thought. Jesus laid aside His right to the wealth of Heaven and came to live among mankind. When He returned to heaven He returned richer than when He had left. How? He now had a relationship with those whom He had redeemed, and we (if we are born again) have been made co-heirs with Him in His riches.

There's a principle here: when we are willing to yield — and actually do yield — our rights to wealth and possessions, we will be able to receive treasures beyond the tangible. To more fully understand this concept, please read the entire passage in this letter, Philippians 2:5-11.

Think with me a moment — how many people do you know whose relationships have been ruined by anger over money or possessions? How many families have been ripped to shreds over how the estate of Mom or Dad was to be divided? How many people have become angry enough over money matters to seek a divorce?

A lady who worked in the credit department of a

jewelry store was confronted by an irate customer. It seems the computer had made a mistake in the billing and subsequent reminder departments. Enough was enough. The customer shouted to the lady, "You have made me so *think*, I can't *mad* straight!"

CHRIST WILLINGLY YIELDED HIS RIGHT TO HIS EXCELLENT REPUTATION

How do you suppose Jesus was treated in heaven as the Son of God? He was the center of worship! He was highly honored! But when He came to this earth, He ". . . made himself nothing" (Phil. 2:7). Christ was born into poverty, in a borrowed stable. Even His hometown had a bad reputation. His birth cast suspicion on Him. His reputation was further damaged by His association with sinners and publicans, and a woman with a sordid past washed His feet. The ultimate damage to His reputation was in His trial and the death reserved for criminals — crucifixion!

One of the strongest inner drives we have as humans is to be approved, accepted, and loved by others. It's important to us how people think and talk about us. We can be affected deeply, even for a lifetime, by what others have said about us.

When Jesus sacrificed His reputation for us and became nothing in obedience to the Heavenly Father, His Father rewarded this obedience and promoted Him with a name that is and will be above every other name.

Dr. Viktor Frankl was imprisoned by the Nazis during World War II because he was a Jew. Previously, his wife, his children, and his parents had been killed in the horror of the holocaust.

The Gestapo made him strip. He stood before them totally naked. Then they cut away his wedding band, his last possession. At that moment, under some of the most difficult circumstances known to any human being, Viktor said to himself, *You can take away my wife, you can take away my children, you can strip me of my clothes and my freedom, but there is one thing no person can EVER take away from me . . . and that is my freedom to choose how I will react to what happens to me!*[2]

CHRIST WILLINGLY YIELDED HIS RIGHT TO BE SERVED

We tend to be selfish, we want to be noticed and doted upon, we want others to wait on us and serve us. Think of the paradox from Christ's life. He was the Creator, the King of all kings. He is equal with God the Father. His name is above all other names. If there ever has been anyone who had the right to be served, it was Jesus.

> *We can be affected deeply, even for a lifetime, by what others have said about us.*

Instead, He chose to yield those rights. He laid them aside in order to serve others, in particular His disciples. When He walked the dusty, dirty roads of Israel, He did it in open sandals in hot weather. He wasn't the only one in open sandals. His followers and all the other people in that day also wore them. It was customary, when guests arrived, for the host to wash their feet. It was an expression of good hospitality, but the task was usually relegated to the lowest servant in a household. Talk about a nasty, smelly, demeaning, humble task. It was a duty often neglected if the servant could get away with it. Apparently this is what had happened the night in the Upper Room. They were ready to eat, but the smell of dirty feet was too much. The washing of the feet had not been done.

Jesus — the Lord of lords — did not look around to find someone to handle this dirty job. Leaving His reputation behind, "He got up from the meal, took off His outer clothing, and wrapped a towel around His waist. After that, He poured water into a basin and began to wash His disciples' feet, drying them with the towel that was wrapped around Him" (John 13:4-5).

Following the object lesson comes the life application: "Do you understand what I have done for you?" He asked the disciples. "You call me 'Teacher' and 'Lord,' and rightly so, for that is what I am. Now that I, your Lord and Teacher, have washed your feet, *you also should wash one another's feet.* I have set you an example that you should do as I have done for you. I tell you the truth, no servant is greater than his master, nor is a messenger greater than the one who sent him. Now that you know these things, *you will be blessed if you do them"* [italics are mine] (John 13:12-17).

Who wouldn't respond to this kind of love action?

This concept doesn't appear only in the Gospels. I found this nugget in Proverbs: "The fear of the Lord teaches a man wisdom, and humility comes before honor" (Prov. 15:33). There is really no other way to receive honor and blessing from God than through this yielding of my right to be served.

It's an old story, but I think it fits here: A man had a dream, and in his dream he went to hell and then to heaven. When he arrived in hell, for the first stop, he noticed all the inhabitants were dirty, unkempt, filthy, and neglected, a condition which didn't surprise him. Then he noticed that all of hell's inhabitants had stiff elbows and their arms were extended without bending, so none of these persons could care for themselves. Then he was transported to heaven. The first thing he noticed was all of the inhabitants in heaven appeared to be happy, well-groomed, clean, and neatly clothed. Upon further close examination, he noticed that all the inhabitants also had the problem of having stiff elbows. The difference is that in heaven, each did what the individual couldn't do for himself/herself. Each was doing the combing of hair, straightening of clothing, washing of the face, and feeding of another!

CHRIST WILLINGLY YIELDED HIS RIGHTS TO THE COMFORTS OF LIFE

Creature comforts are one of those inalienable rights in the American mindset and lifestyle. Have you noticed how all of our society is geared to coddling the creature? We love to be "just right." Too hot — turn on the air conditioning. Too cold — turn up the furnace. Too much work — switch on the labor saving device. Oh, how we love those creature comforts!

There were times when Christ availed himself and His disciples of the fine pleasures of a nice meal and gracious hospitality. Yet more often than not, He denied himself these and slept in the open, walked instead of riding donkeyback, preached in the open air, and sailed the stormy waters of Galilee. Just the fact that He fell asleep in a smelly fishing boat in a storm is some indication of how weary He must have been. He lived without a home.

The Anacostia section of Washington, DC, sits on a bluff overlooking the capital city. Just across the river from the imposing Capitol itself, Anacostia — a ghetto of hunger, war, crime, drugs, and hopelessness — might as well be a continent away. None of Washington's celebrities and power brokers, nor the reporters who track them, cross that natural divide.

However, one balmy June morning in 1981 proved the exception. Black limousines and television camera trucks lined the curb in front of the old red brick Assumption Catholic Church in the heart of Anacostia.

Soon after the cameras and reporters were in place, a small group of nuns and priests arrived, clustered about a wisp of a woman in a white muslin sari. The tiny figure moved with unusual grace up the steps of the church, waving at a cluster of children nearby, and brushing past the reporters crowding the doorway.

This celebrity, who somehow managed to understate her own arrival, an attitude unheard of in a city that thrives on pomp and protocol, was a seventy-three-year-old Albanian nun named Theresa Bojaxhiu — better known as Mother Theresa. As 1979 Nobel Prize winner and a world-famous figure she could have commanded an airport welcome by a host of government bigwigs, addressed a joint session of Congress, or attracted thousands at one of the city's great cathedrals. Instead, she went as inconspicuously as possible to a troubled and neglected corner of the city to establish an outpost for nine of her Sisters of Charity.

Since Mother Theresa wouldn't come to them, the power brokers had to come to her. The mayor and city officials trailed the press into the stark church hall with its chipped and cracked plaster walls. The press, which cultivates its irreverence for politicians, was more restrained with this little woman from the streets of Calcutta. Still, she had to dodge the boom mikes coming at her like spears.

"What do you hope to accomplish here?" someone shouted.

"The joy of loving and being loved," she smiled, her eyes sparkling in the face of the camera lights.

"That takes a lot of money, doesn't it?" another reporter threw out the obvious question. Everything in Washington costs money, and the more it costs the more important it is.

Mother Theresa shook her head, "No, it takes a lot of sacrifice."[3]

CHRIST WILLINGLY YIELDED HIS RIGHT TO VOICE HIS OWN DECISIONS

Could this be the toughest of the "rights" to yield — the making of our own decisions and being able to voice them? There's great pride in being able to announce to the world that "I am a self-made man!" Yet holding on to this right can destroy the relationship we are attempting to build up.

Please don't confuse "rights" with "responsibilities," either. A right is a legal demand which one person can make of another or others, with the expectation that it will be forthcoming. In the name of a "right" lots of things can be demanded of others.

Responsibilities are the opportunities placed upon us so that we can in turn fulfill the God-given rights of others. It's our responsibility to love others. If we concentrate on our responsibilities to others it will allow them to receive, experience and enjoy some of the rights given to them by God. They in turn are freed to fulfill their responsibilities to us so that we may enjoy our God-given rights. If we protect and concentrate on our own rights we break this cycle and cause resentment toward ourselves.

One of the primary causes of anger is the fighting for our own rights. Anger comes when these are denied us. Love doesn't react to rights violated by showing anger. Much of what I have been writing is illustrated in the following:

Some 45 years ago a clergyman was sitting in his office. Unknown to him, several blocks away, a bank was being robbed by three men. As they departed from the bank, one of the robbers shot and killed a teller. Attempting a getaway in their car they encountered mechanical problems only a few blocks from the bank. Leaving the car, they made their way into the church where the pastor was located. The three men came with mixed emotions. One wanted a hostage, one hoped for some help, and the last one was unsure of his motives. With guns in their hand they encountered the preacher. Being disturbed by the intrusion, the preacher attempted to calm them. Then the phone rang and they told him to answer it.

For unknown reasons, as he was talking on the phone, they attacked him with fists and guns. He fell to the floor and they continued their beating. When they thought him dead they lifted his body and began the process of stuffing it behind a radiator that extended out from the wall. They managed to wedge most of his body behind the metal heater, but one of the robbers in a frenzy began to beat the preacher's head and face with a gun. He stopped when he realized the head could not be wedged any further. The assault had removed one of the victim's eyes. They ran.

Minutes later, law enforcement officers came to the study. Seeing evidence of a struggle they discovered the broken body behind the radiator. They ripped the heater from the wall and discovered there was still some life. They rushed the preacher to the hospital. Emergency surgery was performed. While in surgery, he ceased showing any signs of life. Equipment then wasn't as sophisticated as today, and procedures were different. They covered him with a sheet. While in the process of filling out the death certificate a nurse came to them and shouted, "Look!" From under the sheet, the man pronounced dead was still alive. The doctors rushed back in and continued the repair.

A year passed before the preacher left the hospital. A physically devasted man, 100 broken bones had mended, and he had been fitted with a glass eye. His face had been partially restored. He returned to his pastorate.

The three had been apprehended and a trial ordered. The robber who had killed the bank teller was sentenced to death. The other two were tried separately and the pastor was a witness and spectator at their trials. They were both found guilty. On the day of sentencing the pastor stood in the courtroom and asked the judge for a point of personal privilege. An unusual request, but it was granted.

The pastor requested that instead of the two being sentenced to prison they be released to his care and custody. He and his wife would take them in and love them like their own sons. He asked the judge for the opportunity to demonstrate what love, forgiveness, and relationship were all about. The court was shocked, yet granted the request on the proviso that if either of them broke the law their prison sentence would be enforced.

The pastor took the two home with him. He did everything he could to create the conditions of love. One of the men couldn't respond except in a negative way. He was arrested again and sentenced to prison.

The other was sullen and non-communicative, but the pastor and his wife continued by word and deed the demonstration of love.

Nearly two years passed. One afternoon a knock came at the study door. The pastor called out, "Come in." In walked the young man. He hurried across the room and leaned across the desk and with tears welling up said, "Under God, you'll never know the way I feel every time I look at you. Don't you realize I was the one who beat out your eye?"

"Yes, I know it was you," the pastor replied. "I was looking at you when you did it."

The man replied, "I need your help! I can't do anything for you, but I can still help others. I want to become a doctor and help people who are blind. Will you help me?"

The pastor stood up, walked around the desk, embraced the young man, and said, "I not only *can* help you, I will. I'll do everything I can to help you become a doctor if that's what you desire."

Today on the West Coast a man performs surgery to aid the visually impaired. And the reason he does is more than forty years ago he took away from another man the most precious gift that the man possessed — not just his sight, but his life. He literally beat him to death. And that same man, in some kind of miraculous recovery, came back from the dead and offered acceptance, forgiveness, love, and the possibility of a whole new life.[4]

What a picture of the love of God. What a picture of the love of a man. And we are told in God's Word to "be imitators of God, therefore, as dearly loved children and live a life of love, just as Christ loved us and gave himself up for us as a fragrant offering and sacrifice" (Eph. 5:1-2).

Love . . . DOES NOT GET ANGRY EASILY!

16

Making Love an Action

A father, home from work, was trying to work through a manual which was required reading and quite heavy. While he was attempting to give it his full attention, his little son kept interrupting him. He would lean against his knees and say, "Daddy, I love you." The father would give him a pat and say rather absentmindedly, "Yes, son, I love you, too," and he would give him a little push away so he could keep on reading. This didn't satisfy the little guy who finally ran to his father and almost shouted, "I LOVE YOU, DADDY!" As he shouted he jumped on his lap and threw his arms around him and gave him a big squeeze, explaining, "And I've just got to *do* something about it!"

As we are maturing, we no longer will be content with the "pat on the head" kind of love or the "small talk" variety of love. It's time for action! Not only is love an action, it's also . . .

A BIBLICAL COMMAND

"Love the Lord your God with all your heart and with all your soul and with all your strength" (Deut. 6:5). This defines the kind of relationship God intended between himself and all mankind. Even though this was not an explicit command among the Ten Commandments (Exod. 20:1-17), Jesus said this is the very essence of those commandments. It is the very central core and foundation of relations with God. This is considered the first and greatest of all commandments — to love your God. The most important one, said Jesus, is this: "Hear, O Israel, the Lord our God, the Lord is one. Love the Lord your God with all your heart and with all your soul and with all your mind and with all your strength" (Mark 12:29-30).

It follows then that if this is the greatest of all the commandments, failure to keep this commandment must be the greatest sin. I don't think the logic is too faulty, do you? Let's take this a bit further. Christ's explanation of the Ten Commandments here is not a condemnation of the unbeliever. It was addressed to the teachers of the law. It's an indictment of today's Christians. How little love we give to God! "With all your heart and with all your soul and with all your mind and with all your strength," said Jesus. We all need this message.

But Jesus didn't stop here. He continued, "The second is this: Love your neighbor as yourself. There is no commandment greater than these" (12:31). Obedience to this command is the essence of really loving God. If we love God, we love His creation, too. These two dimensions are linked together — love God, love His people. Love people, love God. These cannot be separated.

John the Beloved ties these two together like this, "We love because he (God) first loved us. If anyone says, I love God, yet hates his brother, he is a liar. For anyone who does not love his brother, whom he has seen, cannot love God whom he has not seen. And he has given us this command: Whoever loves God must also love his brother" (1 John 4:19-21). These two commandments are like blossom and fruit, they are inseparable. There cannot be one without the other.

Here is the pivotal point for all of Christianity — it's the essence of what Christians are all about. Jesus concludes, "All the Law and the Prophets hang on these two commandments" (Matt. 22:40). All the Law? All the Commandments? Yes! When we disobey and fail to keep the first we are unable to keep the second. I have quickly concluded that without the grace and mercy of God I cannot keep either of these. How desperately we need a Saviour to save us from ourselves! It's God who creates within us the capacity to love.

"Dear friends, let us love one another, *for love comes from God.* Whoever does not love does not know God, because God is love. This is how God showed his love among us: He sent His one and only Son into the world that we might live through Him. *This is love:* not that we loved God, but that he loved us and sent His Son as an atoning sacrifice for our sins. Dear friends, since God so loved us, *we also ought to love one another.* No one has ever seen God; *but if we love one another,* God lives in us and His love is made complete in us" [italics are mine] (1 John 4:7-12). John gives us the source of our love as well as the secret to sharing it with those around us. If we love, God lives in us and He is made real in human flesh to others. I don't understand this exchange; I only know we are commanded to love, and the way in which this can be a possibility comes out of my relationship with God.

During the Korean War, a South Korean Christian civilian was arrested by the Communists and ordered shot. But when the young Communist leader learned the prisoner was in charge of an orphanage, caring for small children, he decided to keep him and kill his son instead. So they took his nineteen-year-old son and shot him right there in front of the Christian man.

Later, the fortunes of war changed and that same young Communist leader was captured by the United Nations forces, tried, and condemned to death. But before the sentence could be carried out, the Christian whose son had been killed came and pleaded for the life of the killer. He declared that this Communist was young, that he really did not know what he was doing. The Christian said, "Give him to me and I will train him."

The UN forces granted the request. The father took the murderer of his boy into his own home and cared for him. Today that young man, formerly a Communist, is a Christian pastor, serving Christ.[1] That's the kind of love that has no explanation other than that it comes from God. It's beyond the normal, human reaction. It's supernatural.

A SELFLESS LOVE

Have you noticed the topics of Christian seminars lately? Prosperity to prophecy, miracles to marriages, healing to holiness are among those best attended. When was the last time you heard about a seminar on the subject of how to better love the Lord? The subject of loving and obeying God is conspicuous by its absence. Instead we spend our time with emotional inner healing, self-love, and self-esteem. Have we added a third commandment to the two Jesus said were all important? Love yourself first, then love God, then love others? It's widely taught that self-love is the key to everything else.

The normal human being is already self-centered, which is one of the major problems of loving. We are already inwardly focused. God, in His Word, is challenging us to take an outward look at others and God. If you would read again some of Christ's teachings on the subject, you will get the idea Jesus was rebuking self-love. He said we spend too much of our time and resources on clothing, feeding, and sheltering ourselves. It's time to give and share some of this bounty with others.

The love of God is neglected, relegated to a secondary position, while self-love comes first. We are seeing an awakening to world evangelization based on something other than love. We must obey the "Great Commission," but at the same time we also need to obey the Great Commandment! There is an awakening in the Church for those around us, such as the unborn (abortion issues), the homeless, the abused, the deprived, and others. We would be much more effective in these actions if we put first our love for God.

There's a real danger that we can go through all the motions without love, and our efforts will amount to nothing except a loud, irritating noise. Hear it again: "If I speak in the tongues of men and of angels, but have not love, I am only a resounding gong or a clanging cymbal.

If I have the gift of prophecy and can fathom all mysteries and all knowledge, and if I have a faith that can move mountains, but have not love, I am nothing. If I give all I possess to the poor and surrender my body to the flames, but have not love, I gain nothing" (1 Cor. 13:1-3).

These are commendable things to do — understand mysteries, develop knowledge, exercise faith, move mountains, give to the poor, and even make great personal, painful sacrifices. Yet, if they are not motivated by an all-consuming love for God, these things are of no value to God or to ourselves. We somehow have buried our love for God under great flurries of activity.

Portraying love is seen in the story L.E. Maxwell told: A group of prospectors set out from Bannock, Montana (then capital of the state) in search of gold. They went through many hardships and several of their little company died en route. Finally, they were overtaken by Indians who stole their good horses, leaving them with only a few limping old ponies. The Indians then threatened them, telling the prospectors to get back to Bannock and stay there, for if they overtook them again they would murder the lot of them.

Defeated, discouraged, and downhearted, the prospectors sought to make their way back to the capital city. On one occasion as they tethered out the limping ponies on a creek side, one of the men casually picked up a little stone from the creek bed.

He called to his companion for a hammer, and upon cracking the rock he said, "It looks as though there may be gold here." Two of them panned gold the rest of the afternoon and managed to realize twelve dollars worth. The entire little company panned gold the next day in the same creek and realized fifty dollars — a great sum in those days.

They said to each other, "We have struck it!"

They made their way back to Bannock and vowed not to breathe a word concerning this gold strike. They were ever so careful to keep

> *If we have really found Jesus Christ and the love of God, we will be unable to conceal the secret.*

their word. They secretively set about re-equipping themselves with supplies for another prospecting trip.

But when they got ready to go back, three hundred men followed them. Who had told on them? No one! The writer of the book, a purely secular columnist, accounted thus for the incident: "Their beaming faces betrayed the secret!"[2]

If we have really found Jesus Christ and the love of God, we will be unable to conceal the secret. The God of love from within the human being will shine out so others will see.

Love is an action, a decision, a commitment to God first, which will in turn manifest itself in our human relationships. Self-love is not the source. God is the source of love because God *is* love!

BASED ON COMMITMENT

Love is not a feeling or an emotion or something transient. Love is a commitment. A commitment that stands through the tests of time, stress, hardship and discouragement.

The cooling off of love is not because of some diabolical scheme or activities that are sinful. There is just a gradual drifting away from an original commitment, replaced by the urgent concerns of living. It's so easy to get caught up with earning a living, going to school, maintaining the house, caring for the car, etc. Gradually, a love commitment is replaced with tolerance, then complaint, mistreatment, and — finally — resignation.

When I make a commitment, I plan to perform something, carry it out, do an action, act upon the decision, practice it on a regular basis, execute an ongoing lifestyle, pursue the objective, and participate personally in reaching the goal. To commit is to act. To commit is to obligate, bind, make liable, engage, decide, determine, and resolve. A commitment should not be lightly entered into. A commitment is serious business.

There is no easy way to deal with commitment. It must be made out of a personal choice, a decision of the will, an act of devotion. The fear of making a commitment is epidemic in our society. Nobody wants to be committed . . . we want to keep our options open. Just look around us. College students are waiting longer and longer to declare their majors. Couples are marrying later, and marrying tentatively with escape clauses. People take jobs and still keep a resume floating around out there. Couples postpone having children so they can retain their options of personal freedoms. What a sad world we have turned this into. Think of all the children who are caught up in the backwash of parents who are pursuing their personal freedoms, keeping options open, and not committing for the long haul.

This lack of commitment is nothing more nor less than selfishness. And our selfishness is hurting our entire world. With the huge numbers of Bible-believing Christians populating our churches today, this world ought to have been turned upside down by this time. But, sad to say, our day has yet to see the kind of impact great numbers of committed Christians could make with an action of love.

A pastor tells the following: "During vacation Bible school my wife had an experience with her primary class that she says she will never forget. Her class was interrupted on Wednesday about an hour before dismissal when a new student was brought in.

"The little boy had one arm missing, and since the class was almost over she had no opportunity to learn any of the details about the cause, or his state of adjustment. She was very nervous and afraid that one of the other children would comment on his handicap and embarrass him. There was no opportunity to caution them, so she proceeded as carefully as possible.

"As the class time came to a close she began to relax. She asked the class to join her in their usual closing ceremony. 'Let's make our churches,' she said, clasping her hands together, fingers interlocked. 'Here's the church and here's the steeple, open the doors and there's . . . .' The awful truth of her own actions struck her. The very thing she had feared the children would do, she had done!

"As she stood there speechless the little girl sitting next to the boy reached over with her left hand and placed it up to his right hand and said, 'Davey, let's make the church together.' "[3]

Not much is going to happen until we team up with God and together make the church. We can make the church what it ought to be, we can make homes what they should be, we can make this world a better place. But it is a choice. Choose to be committed to love!

Epilogue

Thanks for staying with me all the way through this book. Reading this book may have taught you about love, but all the knowledge you can acquire will amount to nothing unless it's translated into an action. It's of no value until you make a commitment to act out the characteristics of love through your life.

The thing about commitment is that no one else can do it for you. It's not a vicarious experience. You must do it for yourself. The ball is in your court. Here, one more time, is the working definition of love we have used: *Love is an action directed to another person that is motivated by our relationship to Jesus Christ and is given freely without a personal reward in mind.*

We have been confronted with one of the great choices of life. To love or not to love; to love in word or to love in action; to live a selfish life or a self-less life; to live for God or to live for self; to live for others or to live for selfish interests. Really, there is no greater reward that can be yours than that which will come back to you from the deep fulfillment which is from a life committed to love.

Make the commitment to love. Make the commitment to love God first, then to love your neighbor as you love yourself. There really is nothing that can change your life as much as this commitment to love, other than perhaps your initial decision to give your life to Jesus Christ. When you are committed and actually practice love, the results will be amazing! Through you, love-starved neighbors, friends, family members, and church members will experience God's love. Lives will be changed — yours as well as theirs. Think of the joy of being a part of God's delivery system for love. You will become a channel of blessing to others. Your life will likely never be the same.

It's amazing, but when we serve as instruments to funnel God's love to another, the process of love simply passing through us, we also change! And in the simplest of terms, we should be nothing more or less than delivery systems for the love of God.

Bob Weber, who served as a president of Kiwanis International, loved to tell this story: He had spoken to a club in a small town and was spending the night with a farmer on the outskirts of the community. He and the farmer were relaxing on the front porch following a farm supper, when the paper boy delivered the evening paper. The boy noticed the farmer's sign: "Puppies for sale." The boy got off his bike and said to the farmer, "How much do you want for the pups, mister?"

"Twenty-five dollars each, son."

Weber saw the boy's face drop. "Well, sir, could I

at least see them anyway?"

The farmer whistled and in a moment the mother dog came bounding around the corner of the house, followed by four of the cutest puppies you ever saw, tails wagging and yipping happily. At last, another pup came straggling around the house, dragging one hind leg.

"What's the matter with that puppy, mister?" the boy asked.

"Well, son, that pup is crippled. We took her to the vet and he took an x-ray. The pup doesn't have a hip joint and that leg will never be right."

To the amazement of both men the boy dropped his bike, reached for his collection bag, and took out a fifty-cent piece. "Please, mister," the boy pleaded, "I want to buy that pup. I'll pay you fifty cents every week until the $25 is paid. Honest I will, mister."

The farmer replied, "But, son, you don't seem to understand. That pup will never be able to run or jump. That pup will be crippled forever. Why in the world would you want such a useless pup as that?"

The boy paused for a bit, then reached down and pulled up his pant leg, exposing a leg brace and leather knee-strap holding a twisted leg. The boy answered, "Mister, that pup is going to need someone who understands her and loves her to help her in life!"

There is a crippled, hurting world out there who needs someone. And in that hurting world there are people, one at a time, who are needing someone who will love them into the kingdom of God in the name of Jesus Christ.

Love Is

Love is the filling from one's own,
    Another's cup;
Love is the daily laying down
    And taking up;
A choosing of the stony path
    Through each new day,
That other feet may tread with ease
    A smoother way.
Love is not blind, but looks abroad
    Through other's eyes;
And asks not, "Must I give?" but
    "May I sacrifice?"
Love hides its grief, that other hearts
    And lips may sing;
And burdened walks, that other lives
    May buoyant wing.
Hast thou a love like this
    Within thy soul?
'Twill crown thy life with bliss
    When thou dost reach the goal.
        Author Unknown

Your life can become the "love oasis" to which people are attracted. A love that is real, genuine, motivated, and born out of a relationship with God. It's the kind of love that will change the world. Think — you could begin a new revolution! A revolution of love, not hate. There is a desperate famine of love — people are literally dying because they cannot find love. The answer? Love — from God through you to needy, hurting people — that is the answer!

Love is patient,
love is kind.
It does not envy,
it does not boast,
it is not proud.
It is not rude,
it is not self-seeking,
it is not easily angered,
it keeps no record of wrongs.
Love does not delight in evil
but rejoices with the truth.
It always protects,
always trusts,
always hopes,
always perseveres.
Love never fails!
And now these three remain:
Faith, hope and love.
But the greatest of these is love!
(1 Cor. 13:4-8,13)

Well, what are you waiting for? The challenge has been given, the need stated. Now is the time, you are the person, this is the place to move into action with love!

Once more, and for the last time . . .

If not *now* . . . when will it be done?
If not *you* . . . who will be the instrument of love?

Notes

Introduction
[1] John Naisbitt, *Megatrends* (New York, NY: Warner Books, 1982).
[2] George Gallup, Jr., *Forecast 2000* (New York, NY: William Morrow & Company, Inc., 1984).

Chapter 1
[1] Harold Myra, *Living By God's Surprises* (Waco, TX: Word, 1988), p. 23.
[2] Courtney Anderson, *To the Golden Shore* (Boston, MA: Little Brown and Company, 1956).

Chapter 2
[1] Rebecca Pippert, *Out of the Saltshaker* (Downers Grove, IL: InterVarsity Press, 1979).

Chapter 3
[1] Dr. Paul Brand and Philip Yancey, *Fearfully and Wonderfully Made* (Grand Rapids, MI: Zondervan Publ. House, 1980), p. 77-79.
[2] George Hunter, *The Contagious Congregation* (Nashville, TN: Abingdon Press, 1979).
[3] Rabbi Mervin Tomski, Temple Emanuel of Burbank, CA.
[4] Warren C. Hamby, *Eight Keys to Happiness* (Old Tappan, NJ: Fleming H. Revell Co., 1969), p. 102-103.

Chapter 6
[1] Win Arn, Carroll Nyquist, and Charles Arn, *Who Cares About Love?* (Monrovia, CA: Church Growth, 1986), adapted, p. 132.
[2] Alan Loy McGinnis, *The Friendship Factor* (Minneapolis, MN: Augsburg Publ. House, 1979), p. 54.
[3] Tony Campolo, *Who Switched the Price Tags?* (Waco, TX: Word Books, 1987).

Chapter 9
[1] Chuck Johnson, *Parables, Etc.*, July 1984 (Saratoga, CA: Saratoga Press).

Chapter 10
[1] Albert Stauderman, *Let Me Illustrate* (Minneapolis, MN: Augsburg Publ. House, 1983), p. 140.
[2] Clifton Fadiman, Editor, *The Little Brown Book of Anecdotes.*

[3] C. S. Lewis, *Mere Christianity* (Greensburg, PA: Barbour and Co., Inc., 1985), p. 109, 114.
[4] The source is unknown, could possibly be a *Reader's Digest* story.

Chapter 11
[1] Gerald G. Jampolsky, M.D., *Love Is Letting Go of Fear* (Millbrae, CA: Celestial Arts, 1979), p. 129.
[2] Richard Selzer, *Mortal Lessons,* p. 45-46.

Chapter 13
[1] Wilbur Rees, *$3.00 Worth of God* (Elgin, IL: David C. Cook Publ. Co., 1979).
[2] *Sunday Sermons,* September/October 1983. (Pleasantville, NJ: Voicings).
[3] Charlie Webster, *Parables, etc.* May 1986 (Saratoga, CA: Saratoga Press).

Chapter 14
[1] Edwin Evans, *Parables, etc.,* June 1984 (Saratoga, CA: Saratoga Press), p. 2.
[2] Earl D. Radmacher, *You and Your Thoughts, The Power of Right Thinking* (Wheaton, IL: Tyndale House Publ., Inc., 1977), p. 15, 19.
[3] John Edmund Haggai, *How to Win over Worry* (Eugene, OR: Harvest House Publ., 1987).

Chapter 15
[1] Paul Lee Tan, *Encyclopedia of 7700 Illustrations* (Garland, TX: Bible Communications, Inc., 1979).
[2] Robert Schuller, *The Be-Happy Attitudes* (Waco, TX: Word Books, 1987), adapted, p. 199.
[3] Charles Colson, *Loving God* (Grand Rapids, MI: Zondervan Publ. House, 1987), p. 126.
[4] Ed Beck, *Parables, etc.,* April 1984 (Saratoga, CA: Saratoga Press).

Chapter 16
[1] *Parables, etc.* September 1983 (Saratoga, CA: Saratoga Press).
[2] L.E. Maxwell, *The Prairie Overcomer,* May 1984, (Canada: Prairie Bible Institute). p. 34.
[3] Jeanie Stoppel, *Parables, etc.,* February 1984 (Saratoga, CA: Saratoga Press).